Access to History

G

Access to History

General Editor: Keith Randell

The Habsburg Empire, 1815-1918

Nick Pelling

Hodder & Stoughton

A MEMBER OF THE HODDER HEADLINE GROUP

The cover illustration is a portrait of Franz Joseph by Julius von Blaas courtesy of the Arts and History Picture Library.

Some other titles in the series:

France: Monarchy, Republic and Empire 1814-70   ISBN 0 340 51805 7
Keith Randell

France: The Third Republic 1870-1914   ISBN 0 340 55569 6
Keith Randell

Russia 1815-81   ISBN 0 340 54789 8
Russell Sherman

Reaction and Revolutions: Russia 1881-1924   ISBN 0 340 53336 6
Michael Lynch

The Unification of Italy 1815-70   ISBN 0 340 51809 X
Andrina Stiles

The Concert of Europe: International Relations 1814-70 ISBN 0 340 53496 6
John Lowe

Rivalry and Accord: International Relations 1870-1914   ISBN 0 340 51806 5
John Lowe

The Unification of Germany 1815-96   ISBN 0 340 51810 3
Andrina Stiles

British Library Cataloguing in Publication Data

A catalogue for this title is available from the British Library

ISBN 0-340-59377-6

First published 1996

Impression number   10 9 8 7 6 5 4 3 2 1
Year   1999   1998   1997   1996

Typeset by Sempringham publishing services, Bedford
Printed in Great Britain for Hodder & Stoughton Educational,
a division of Hodder Headline Plc, 338 Euston Road, London NW1 3BH
by Redwood Books, Trowbridge, Wiltshire

Contents

Preface

To the general reader

Although the *Access to History* series has been designed with the needs of students studying the subject at higher examination levels very much in mind, it also has a great deal to offer the general reader. The main body of the text (i.e. ignoring the Study Guides at the ends of chapters) forms a readable and yet stimulating survey of a coherent topic as studied by historians. However, each author's aim has not merely been to provide a clear explanation of what happened in the past (to interest and inform): it has also been assumed that most readers wish to be stimulated into thinking further about the topic and to form opinions of their own about the significance of the events that are described and discussed (to be challenged). Thus, although no prior knowledge of the topic is expected on the reader's part, she or he is treated as an intelligent and thinking person throughout. The author tends to share ideas and possibilities with the reader, rather than passing on numbers of so-called 'historical truths'.

To the student reader

There are many ways in which the series can be used by students studying History at a higher level. It will, therefore, be worthwhile thinking about your own study strategy before you start your work on this book. Obviously, your strategy will vary depending on the aim you have in mind, and the time for study that is available to you.

If, for example, you want to acquire a general overview of the topic in the shortest possible time, the following approach will probably be the most effective:

1 Read Chapter 1 and think about its contents.
2 Read the 'Making notes' section at the end of Chapter 2 and decide whether it is necessary for you to read this chapter.
3 If it is, read the chapter, stopping at each heading to note down the main points that have been made.
4 Repeat stage 2 (and stage 3 where appropriate) for all the other chapters.

If, however, your aim is to gain a thorough grasp of the topic, taking however much time is necessary to do so, you may benefit from carrying out the same procedure with each chapter, as follows:

1 Read the chapter as fast as you can, and preferably at one sitting.
2 Study the flow diagram at the end of the chapter, ensuring that you understand the general 'shape' of what you have just read.

3 Read the 'Making notes' section (and the 'Answering essay questions' section, if there is one) and decide what further work you need to do on the chapter. In particularly important sections of the book, this will involve reading the chapter a second time and stopping at each heading to think about (and to write a summary of) what you have just read.

4 Attempt the 'Source-based questions' section. It will sometimes be sufficient to think through your answers, but additional understanding will often be gained by forcing yourself to write them down.

When you have finished the main chapters of the book, study the 'Further Reading' section and decide what additional reading (if any) you will do on the topic.

This book has been designed to help make your studies both enjoyable and successful. If you can think of ways in which this could have been done more effectively, please write to tell me. In the meantime, I hope that you will gain greatly from your study of History.

Keith Randell

Acknowledgements

The Publishers would like to thank the following for permission to reproduce illustrations in this volume:

Cover - courtesy of Arts and History Picture Library; Mansell Collection, p. 15; British Museum, p. 50; Private Collection/Bridgeman Art Library, London, p. 123.

Text acknowledgements

Penguin Ltd for the extract from *The Habsburg Monarchy 1809-1918* by A J P Taylor (1948); Macmillan Ltd for the extract from *The Fall of the House of Habsburg* by E Crankshaw (1963); Longmans Ltd for the extract from *The Decline and Fall of the Habsburg Empire* by A Sked (1989) and *The Dissolution of the Habsburg Empire* by J N Mason; Weidenfeld and Nicolson Ltd for the extract from *The Habsburg Empire* by C A Macartney; Holt, Rinehart and Winston for the extract from *The Habsburg Legacy* by B Parley.

Every effort has been made to trace and acknowledge ownership of copyright. The publishers will be glad to make suitable arrangements with any copyright holders whom it has not been possible to contact.

CHAPTER 1

Introduction: The Habsburg Empire, 1815-1918

The Habsburgs were the most successful dynasty in modern history. Over a period of some six hundred years they built around the small archduchy of Austria a huge empire covering about 250,000 square miles and containing at least eleven different nationalities. From the sixteenth to the early twentieth century this empire dominated central and eastern European history. But, in the summer of 1914, the Empire which had lasted so long and become so grand was suddenly, violently jolted into a world war which would destroy it.

The critical event occurred on 28 June 1914. On that pleasant summer day Archduke Franz Ferdinand, heir to the Austrian throne, made a state visit to Sarajevo - capital of the Habsburg province of Bosnia. Unfortunately, as the Archduke's open-topped car made its way through the streets of Sarajevo the chauffeur took a wrong turning into a narrow side street and then decided to reverse. In so doing he manoeuvred the Habsburg Empire backwards into oblivion. On the pavement as the car drew slowly alongside was a young student by the name of Gavrilo Princip, a nineteen-year-old Bosnian Serb who had come to Sarajevo specifically to kill the heir to the Habsburg throne.

Princip was working for a Serbian terrorist organisation, known as the Black Hand, which wanted to see the Habsburgs forced out of Bosnia and the province absorbed into Serbia. But as an assassin Princip was rather incompetent, as indeed were the friends he enlisted to help him with his task. Earlier that day the would-be assassins had enjoyed ample opportunity to kill their man as he cruised slowly through the main streets. But one young man was too frightened to throw his bomb. Another managed to knock the detonator off his bomb as he threw it. Yet another decided not to attempt the assassination because he felt sorry for the Archduke's wife. Finally, Princip went off in disgust to contemplate suicide.

Some time later the dejected Princip became aware that the car reversing slowly towards him had the Archduke within it. At this point Princip jumped onto the running board and murdered Franz Ferdinand with a single revolver shot from extremely close range. For some reason he also fired a second shot which took the life of the Archduke's beautiful wife Sophie.

This bizarre turn of events led directly to the outbreak of the First World War which in turn led to the dissolution of the Habsburg Empire. It is therefore tempting to conclude that the Habsburg Empire was destroyed because a chauffeur took a wrong turn. However, this would, of course, be simplistic. The Empire was facing numerous domestic and foreign threats to its position even before Princip squeezed the trigger.

But in order to understand the problems faced by the Habsburgs in the modern period it is vital to have an understanding of the historical development of the Empire before that time.

1 The Historical Background

The Habsburgs were in origin a minor Germanic noble family. The name itself is a contraction of the name of an eleventh-century Swiss castle in the possession of the family, known as the 'Habichtsburg' or 'Castle of Hawks'. The rise of this family to Great Power status occurred gradually between the thirteenth and sixteenth centuries. The first significant steps towards greatness were undoubtedly taken during the reign of Rudolph I, Count of Habsburg. In 1273 Rudolph was elected Holy Roman Emperor, a title which conferred considerable influence on the family and which they were to hold for all but a few years until Napoleon abolished the Holy Roman Empire in 1806. Perhaps more importantly, in 1278 Rudolph fought for and won the archduchy of Austria and the lands around Vienna, which were to make up the heart of the future great empire.

In the fourteenth century the Habsburgs continued to add territories to the Austrian nucleus. But in the fifteenth and sixteenth centuries,

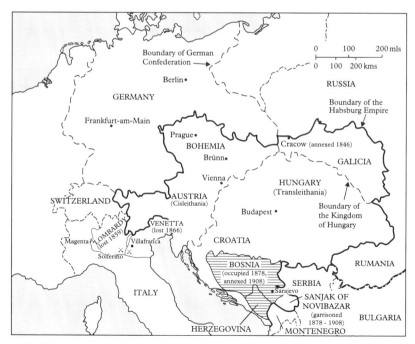

The Habsburg Empire 1815-1918

thanks to a deliberate policy of marrying into families which could offer territorial gain, there was a dramatic escalation in size and status. The mastermind behind this development was the Emperor Maximilian I. In the early sixteenth century Maximilian arranged a marriage between his granddaughter Mary and the King of Bohemia and Hungary. The kingdoms of Bohemia and Hungary were far greater than their names suggest. The Kingdom of Bohemia brought with it Moravia and Silesia. The Kingdom of Hungary brought with it Transylvania and the Kingdom of Croatia, including Slavonia and Dalmatia. In 1526 the King of Bohemia was killed by the Turks at the battle of Mohács and all his possessions passed into the hands of the Habsburgs. Maximilian had, by a combination of marital gambles and good luck, created the basis of a great central and eastern European state.

But the empire of the early sixteenth century differed quite markedly from the future Habsburg Empire in one very important respect. Maximilian had also married his way into vast territorial inheritances in western Europe. In the first half of the sixteenth century the Habsburgs dominated not only central Europe but *all* of Europe. Maximilian's grandson, Charles V, inherited an Empire that made him sovereign in Spain, the Netherlands, large parts of Italy, the Holy Roman Empire, Hungary, Bohemia and the so-called New World in the Americas. For a brief period the Habsburgs pursued the medieval ideal of a united Christendom ruled over by the twin authorities of Pope and Holy Roman Emperor.

But such an unwieldy empire soon proved beyond the abilities of one man to govern, and in 1556 the Emperor Charles V abdicated as Holy Roman Emperor and divided his dominions roughly into two halves: a western empire dominated by Spain and an Austrian empire with Vienna at its heart. This then was the real beginning of the Habsburg Empire that was to determine the balance of power in central Europe for the next 360 years. In the seventeenth century, whilst the Spanish Habsburg Empire went into slow decline, the Austrian Empire emerged as a truly great power. The dynasty carved out a role for itself as the most staunch defender of Roman Catholicism in Europe, leading the so-called Counter Reformation. This was also the period when so much of the wonderful Baroque architecture of the Empire was created as the arts were employed to glorify simultaneously both God and the Habsburgs.

The eighteenth century saw the ideals of the Counter Reformation give way to the ideas of the Enlightenment. Empress Maria Theresa (1740-80) and her son, Emperor Joseph II (1780-90), are both frequently described as 'Enlightened Despots'. This means that, although they ruled in the traditional autocratic fashion, they sought to make the government and administration of the Empire as efficient and reasonable as possible. As a result, this period saw numerous 'enlightened' reforms. Most importantly of all, the administration of the

Empire was centralised in Vienna, under a rapidly expanding bureaucracy. This particular reform, though prompted by the desire for greater efficiency, turned the governing of the Empire into a painfully slow business.

The Enlightenment did not stop the eighteenth century also being a century of wars for the Habsburgs. As a result of war and diplomatic activity they both won and lost territory. The War of the Spanish Succession (1702-14) brought them the Spanish Netherlands. The war of the Austrian Succession saw them lose Silesia to Prussia - an ominous development which foreshadowed the struggle that was to come between the Empire and Prussia in the nineteenth century for dominance in Germany. The destruction of Poland in three partitions negotiated with Prussia and Russia brought the north-eastern Polish provinces of Galicia and Bukovina. At the end of the century came the wars against revolutionary France. In a sense it is here that the modern history of the Habsburgs begins. The French Revolution gave force to the ideas of nationalism and liberalism. In his own way, Napoleon exported these ideas which threatened the very existence of the Habsburg state which was both illiberal and multi-ethnic.

But by 1815 the Empire had helped to defeat the French and the wars were at an end, and yet the ideas unleashed by the Revolution were not

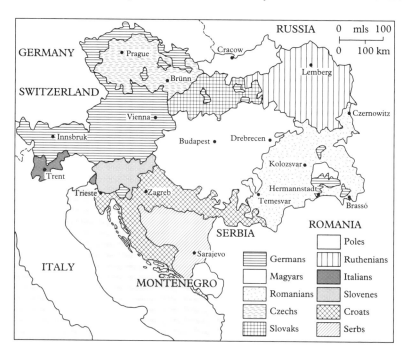

Nationalities in the Habsburg Empire

so easily vanquished. Indeed, it might well be argued that the Empire was to spend the next hundred years trying and eventually failing either to eradicate or to assimilate the ideas of the Revolution.

2 The Peoples of the Habsburg Empire

For many historians the multi-ethnic nature of the Habsburg Empire is the key to understanding its history. But in order to grasp fully the complexity of the so-called 'nationalities problem' it is vital to know something about the nature of each distinct group.

a) The Germans

The Germans were the dominant racial group within the Empire. The dynasty itself was German in origin and the German language was the language of the court and the state bureaucracy and therefore of power. In 1910 the Germans were recorded as making up 23 per cent of the population of the Empire. Though this may seem a low percentage it still made them the biggest single ethnic group.

However the ascendancy of the Germans was profoundly changed in 1867 when a new constitution, known as the *Ausgleich* (Compromise), divided the Empire into two halves: the German aristocracy continued to be the ruling class in the west (Cisleithania) but the Hungarians (Magyars) became the dominant group in the east (Transleithania). Thus after 1867 it is true to say that there were two ruling nationalities in the so-called Austro-Hungarian Empire.

b) The Magyars

Next to the Germans, both in terms of numbers and influence, came the Hungarians, more correctly known as Magyars, who made up around 20 per cent of the population in 1910. After the creation of Austria-Hungary in 1867 they became in effect equal partners in the business. In fact the number of people officially recorded as Hungarian rose sharply after 1867, due to the policy of 'Magyarisation' by which people were pressurised into adopting Hungarian identity. Whilst the Germans found it increasingly difficult to maintain their dominance in the west, after 1867 the Magyars established a fierce grip on their half of the Empire.

c) The Slav Groups

It is common to refer to the bulk of the other peoples of the Empire as Slavs. However, although this is in some ways accurate, such a way of describing the ethnic structure of the empire can be quite misleading.

For example, it is true that in 1910 the Slavs made up 45 per cent of the entire population. This means that the Slavs were by far the biggest single bloc of people. One might therefore assume that the Slavs would have been an enormously powerful group, and yet they were not. The reason for this is quite simple: the Slavs were not united. In fact the reverse was true. They did not feel a common sense of identity, and politically they were more often rivals than allies. For this reason it will be necessary to say something about each Slav group in turn.

i) The Czechs

The Czechs were the largest single Slav group, making up 12 per cent of the Imperial population. The Czech lands, originally the medieval Kingdom of St. Wenceslas, consisted of Bohemia, Moravia and parts of Silesia. Unlike almost all other Slav territories, it gradually became, in the course of the nineteenth century, a very wealthy area as a result of industrialisation. This in turn meant that, again unlike other Slav areas, there was a developed middle class prepared to use its power to advance the nationalist cause. Hence from 1848 to 1918 the Habsburgs always faced the challenge of a powerful Czech nationalist movement. However, the nationalists never asked for complete separation from the Empire; their main aim was to create a federal constitution in which the Czechs might achieve a similar status to the Magyars.

ii) The Poles

The Poles, although only 10 per cent of the total population, were the fourth largest ethnic group. They lived predominantly in Galicia, beyond the Carpathian mountains in the remote north-east of the Empire. Naturally the Poles within the Habsburg Empire resented the fact that Austria, Russia and Prussia had carved up and shared out all of what had been Poland between them, and in the first half of the nineteenth century they were involved in sporadic revolts and rebellions aimed at furthering their ultimate aim of recreating an independent homeland.

However, after the failure of these tactics, the Poles adopted a different approach. In 1868 they declared their loyalty to the Monarchy. As a result of this the Habsburgs allowed them almost complete rights of self-government in their province of Galicia, though no doubt the decision was also influenced by the fact that the province was too remote to be governed effectively from Vienna. Thus, in the second half of the century the political role of the Poles underwent a curious *volte-face*, changing from opponents to supporters of the status quo.

iii) The Ruthenians

In some ways the real victims of this arrangement were the Ruthenians, who shared much of Galicia and neighbouring Bukovina with the Poles.

The political dominance of the Poles in Galicia was very much at the expense of the Ruthenians. Although the Poles only fractionally outnumbered the Ruthenians, the electoral system had been deliberately designed to make sure that the provincial parliament was always heavily dominated by Poles. However, although this may sound like a recipe for Ruthenian revolt, this was not the case. The Ruthenian nationalist movement was slow to gain momentum in the nineteenth century, largely due to the fact that most of the Ruthenians were impoverished peasants who had little time for political activities. Nevertheless, when the Emperor introduced universal suffrage in the western half of the Empire in 1907, the Poles felt compelled to adjust their provincial franchise to allow the Ruthenians greater access to the political system in Galicia. By 1914 the Ruthenians, though not entirely satisfied, were fundamentally loyal to the dynasty.

iv) The Croats

The Croats, though only 5 per cent of the total population, gradually carved out a position of considerable influence for themselves within the structure of the Empire. Before 1867 they had tended to support the centralised rule of Vienna as something preferable to being ruled over by the Magyars. For their part the Magyars always claimed that Croatia fell within the ancient Kingdom of St. Stephen and indeed the *Ausgleich* of 1867 placed Croatia firmly within the Magyar half of the Empire. But, in the next year, the Croats made their own compromise with the Magyars, known as the *Nagodba*, and as a result came to enjoy privileges similar to the Poles, namely a significant degree of self-government within Croatia. But this did not entirely put a stop to a Croatian-led movement which aimed at creating an independent south Slav state consisting of Croatians, Serbs and Slovenes. Although this movement would appear to foreshadow the emergence of Yugoslavia, before 1914 it was very weak and internally divided.

v) The Serbs

The position of the Serbs within the Empire was yet more complex. Before 1878 they were a very small group of roughly 750,000 distributed unevenly in Croatia and Dalmatia. But in 1878 all this changed. The Congress of Berlin sanctioned Austrian occupation of Bosnia and Herzegovina, and as a result the Serbian population of the Empire was suddenly more than doubled. More worryingly, the Congress also recognised the existence of Serbia as a newly independent state bordering on Bosnia. There can be little doubt that Serbia was an expansionist power with designs on Bosnian Serb territory as part of its mission to create a Greater Serbia. Again this might be said to foreshadow the eventual creation of Yugoslavia, but it should be pointed out that the idea of a Greater Serbia was most definitely not welcomed by the Croats.

vi) The Slovenes

The smallest of the south Slav peoples were the Slovenes. They were largely a peasant population, frequently described as conservative, Catholic and basically loyal to the Empire. Towards the end of the century a Slovene nationalist movement did develop but its aims were strictly limited, such as trying to establish rights to use the Slovene language in schools.

vii) The Slovaks

The last Slav group within the Empire was the Slovaks, occupying the lands to the east of the Czech provinces. Making up only 4 per cent of the total population, most of whom were once again poor peasants, it would be fair to say that their political influence was negligible. After 1867 they found themselves in the Hungarian half of the Empire and thus cut off from the Czechs. As a result the Czechs and the Slovaks did not have much chance for political co-operation and therefore the idea of a separate Czecho-Slovak state had little or no currency before 1914.

d) Non-Slav Groups

In addition to the various Slav groups, the Empire also contained Italians and Romanians.

i) The Italians

The Italians were for almost the first sixty years of the century a particularly troublesome group. Italian nationalism was a powerful and almost irresistible force in Italy and motivated many Italians within the Habsburg Empire, particularly in Lombardy and Venetia, to seek to join the emerging new state of Italy. But this problem was radically transformed between 1859 and 1866. In 1859 the Habsburgs were forced to relinquish Lombardy, and in 1866 Venetia was also lost: both to the new state of Italy. Although there was some loss of face in this, after 1866 the remaining Italians within the Empire, in South Tyrol and along the Dalmatian coastline, were too few in number to prove a significant problem. More to the point, the possibility that the Habsburgs might at some point concede these areas to Italy actually helped to improve relations between Italy and Austria-Hungary. Between 1882 and 1914 they were allies. But in 1915 Italy suddenly entered the war against Austria-Hungary because the western allies secretly but insincerely promised Italy significant territorial gains after Austria's defeat.

ii) The Romanians

Although making up 6.5 per cent of the population, the Romanians were not a great problem for the Empire. Inhabiting Transylvania in the far east of the Empire, they were too remote to cause many headaches in Vienna. Politically they were also rather isolated. Although it is true that an independent Romania came to border on Habsburg Transylvania in the second half of the nineteenth century, the new Romania did not seek to redeem the 'lost' territories, but instead deliberately renounced them in order to retain Austria-Hungary as an ally.

iii) Jews and Muslims

We have now looked at the eleven ethnic groups that make up the standard list of the peoples of the Habsburg Empire. But something should be said of two ostensibly religious groups which also had a sense of separate identity. First, there were the Jews. Although just under 5 per cent of the population, they had a very disproportionate influence. This was because their communities tended to be concentrated in the larger cities. For example, the Jews made up 12 per cent of the population of Vienna by 1914. In addition to this, although Jews could be found in almost any walk of life, they dominated banking and were astonishingly successful in the middle-class professions. In Vienna in the 1880s 61 per cent of the doctors were of Jewish origin, as were 57 per cent of the lawyers. Jews, such as Freud and Mahler, also made a quite exceptional contribution to the cultural flowering of Vienna at the turn of the century. However, although the Jews were increasingly the victim of anti-semitism as the century neared its close, as a community they made great efforts to adopt the language and culture of the dominant Germans. In that sense, although the Jews continued to practise their religion, their desire to be assimilated into the life of the Empire meant that they did not form part of a nationalist movement.

Finally, there was the Muslim community. When the Empire occupied Bosnia-Herzegovina in 1878 it gained a small Bosnian community of Muslims. Although at first they attempted to resist Austrian Imperialist rule, the Muslims were eventually reconciled to the regime. This was partly due to sheer force but also because the Habsburg authorities introduced something approximating to law and order into what had been an almost lawless outpost of the crumbling Ottoman Empire. More importantly, the Habsburgs allowed the Muslims, and indeed the Orthodox Serbs and Catholic Croats, who made up the remainder of the population of Bosnia-Herzegovina, complete religious freedom. Perhaps surprisingly, given the wars of the late twentieth century, there appears to have been relatively little religious or ethnic conflict between Bosnian Muslims, Serbs or Croats in the late nineteenth century.

3 The History of the Habsburg Empire in the Modern Period

The history of the Empire between the fall of Napoleon in 1815 and the dissolution of the Empire in 1918 can be broadly divided into five phases.

The first clear phase is the period between the fall of Napoleon in 1815 and the wave of European revolutions in 1848. This period is frequently referred to as the Age of Metternich, taking its name from the Emperor's influential chancellor. Metternich was a deeply conservative politician who devoted himself to the suppression of any movements or ideas which seemed likely to lead to the re-emergence of revolution. He did this within the Habsburg Empire by creating what some historians refer to as a police state. But he is more well known as the 'policeman of Europe': the mastermind behind a system of alliances in Europe dedicated to the preservation of the restored *Ancien Régime*.

The second phase begins in March 1848 when revolutionary upheavals in Vienna forced Metternich to resign. For a brief period the Empire was rocked by a sequence of revolutions in the major provincial capitals. But the Age of Revolution was short lived. By the end of 1849 all the revolutions were suppressed.

The period between the suppression of the revolutions and the creation of the so-called Dual Monarchy in 1867 can be seen as a third distinct phase in the modern history of the Empire. It is best thought of as a prolonged period of identity crisis: a time when the Empire seemed unable to define a clear role for itself either in Europe or in terms of its domestic constitution. The latter was repeatedly changed in these years as the Empire lurched from crisis to crisis. The biggest of those crises was the military defeat by Prussia in 1866. However, in the next year, partly as a result of the defeat, the Emperor agreed to the creation of the *Ausgleich* or Compromise, by which the Hungarians were allowed to govern the eastern half of the Empire and the Austrians the west. After 1867 historians commonly refer to the Empire as the Austro-Hungarian Empire or the Dual Monarchy. It was a peculiar constitutional arrangement but one which was to the last until the end of the entire Empire.

The *Ausgleich* provided considerable political stability and as a result the history of the Empire between 1867 and the outbreak of world war in 1914 appears to have a certain continuity. This fourth phase in the history of the Habsburgs in the modern period is characterised by growing tensions in the Balkans and the rise of nationalism amongst the peoples of the Empire. The assassination of the heir to the Habsburg throne and the beginning of the Great War mark the dramatic end of this long period.

Finally the last phase in the history of the Empire is the war itself. It is often assumed that the Empire disintegrated rapidly once war had begun. This is not so. In order to understand why the allies dissolved the Habsburg Empire it is necessary to study the war years quite closely.

4 The Habsburgs and the Historians

Most historians writing about the Habsburg Empire between 1815 and 1918 have concentrated on one familiar theme: decline and fall. So much does the history of this Empire appear to be a story of impending doom that historians have, for the most part, restricted themselves to explaining why this fate was so inevitable.

Within the historiography that sets out to delineate this decline it is possible to identify two main schools of thought. Firstly there are those like Oscar Jászi in his seminal work, *The Dissolution of the Habsburg Monarchy* (1929), who argue that the rise of nationalism was a sentence of death upon an Empire consisting of at least eleven different ethnic groups. The second school of thought focuses less on internal problems and more on foreign policy trends. Perhaps the most influential historian in this crowded field has been A.J.P. Taylor whose classic work, *The Habsburg Monarchy 1809-1918,* still remains the best narrative history of the subject written by any British historian. According to Taylor, the Habsburg Monarchy collapsed because it allowed itself to become the ally of Germany at a time when German foreign policy was reckless and bellicose.

However, these two schools have not gone entirely unchallenged. In recent years a revisionist approach has become more noticeable which has been largely dominated (in terms of the output of English speaking academics at least) by Alan Sked. Of particular importance to any student of the Habsburg Empire is Sked's, *The Decline and Fall of the Habsburg Empire 1815-1918,* (actually an odd title given his argument, as you will see).

Although Sked is a former pupil of Taylor's and retains enormous respect for his work, it seems that he does not accept the idea that the Empire was inevitably doomed to fail. According to Sked we must remember that 'the fact that the Monarchy fell does not logically imply any decline at all'. Indeed Sked is at pains to argue that after the 1848 revolutions the Empire 'rose rather than declined'. The dissolution of the Empire thus becomes a sudden death, brought about by the extraordinary circumstances of war, which were by their very nature out of keeping with all that had gone before.

Obviously you should try to read the books referred to for yourself. But you will also find it helpful to read the last chapter of this book which contains an extended discussion of the strengths and weaknesses of these views and a look at a more cultural interpretation of the problems facing the Habsburg Empire.

Working on '*Introduction: the Habsburg Empire, 1815-1918*'

As you work on this subject you will no doubt be impressed with the considerable complexity of the topic. The history of the Habsburg Empire is not the history of one nation: it is the history of several and therefore more than normally complex. It is therefore vital to approach the subject with patience and try not to look for easy answers. It may be comforting to know that one of the greatest historians of the subject, A.J.P. Taylor, was not put off the subject even after a senior academic adviser told him that in order to write a history of the Habsburg Empire he would 'only need to know seventeen languages and live ten times as long as mortal man'.

Armed with patience and a little scepticism your first concrete task will be to familiarise yourself with the main issues within any given topic. This will require careful reading and noting. You next task will be to grasp what historians have argued about any given issue. You will need to discover the main points on which historians have disagreed and be aware of the evidence that can be used for and against any particular view. Finally your most diffcult task will be to arrive at conclusions of your own about the issues you have studied. This will be difficult, especially when it is remembered that professional historians do not necessarily agree. You may feel that you are not in a position to take a definite viewpoint. Although this is acceptable, you should not climb on to the fence too readily.

This book is only intended as a thorough introduction to a difficult topic. You should always try to read more widely and this is often best done when you are trying to get more information about one incident or moment. Remember that often the real pleasure of studying history lies in formulating and testing your own views, not in slavishly reiterating the views of others.

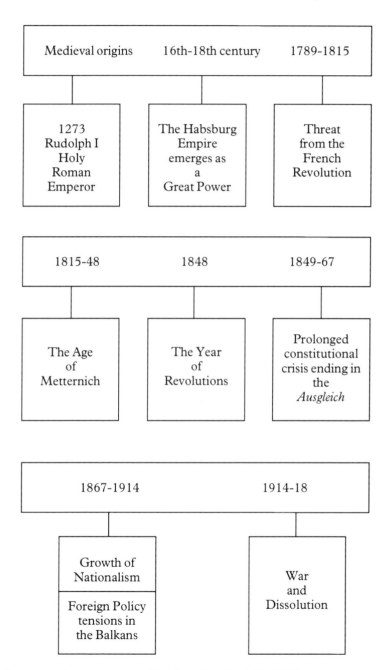

Summary - Introduction: the Habsburg Empire, 1815-1918

CHAPTER 2

The Age of Metternich

The period 1815 to 1848 is often referred to simply as the Age of Metternich. He was undoubtedly the single most influential minister in Habsburg affairs in these years, being foreign minister from 1809 and simultaneously chancellor (the leading minister) from 1821 until his fall in 1848. But his importance extends far beyond the boundaries of the Empire. He is frequently cast as the mastermind behind the general restoration of the *Ancien Régime* in Europe after the great upheavals caused by the French Revolution and the Napoleonic Wars (1789-1815).

Historians often state that Metternich imposed his 'system' on Europe. Put simply, the idea is that Metternich geared all his policies, domestic and foreign, to the preservation of absolute monarchy, the social dominance of the aristocracy and the suppression of the two great ideological legacies of the French Revolution: liberalism and national-ism. The argument is that the success of the system can be measured by the fact that, guided by Metternich, Europe enjoyed 33 years of conservative stability after one of the most profoundly revolutionary periods in modern history.

1 Metternich: Background and Character

What kind of a man was it that could so dominate European history for more than a generation? Metternich's social origins reveal a great deal about his approach to politics. He was born into the high German nobility in 1773 at Coblenz in the Rhineland. His father was a Count of the Holy Roman Empire and devoted his life to the service of the Habsburgs in their capacity as Holy Roman Emperors. In 1794 the Metternich family was forced to move to Vienna to escape the French invasion of the Rhineland. This first brush with the Revolution had a profound impact on the younger Metternich and his later devotion to the suppression of revolution can, in part, be explained as the result of his personal memory of the chaos and upheaval brought by revolution. Ironically the enforced move to Vienna proved to be a good thing for Metternich's career. He began to mix with the ruling elite, the Austrian aristocracy, and when he joined the Habsburg diplomatic service in 1801 his new social connections enabled him to climb rapidly to the top.

It might be expected that a man who devoted himself to the prevention of change and the suppression of ideas would be a rather uncomplicated and authoritarian figure, but this was not the case. Metternich was a complex and contradictory personality. He regarded himself, with good cause, as the greatest politician of his age and saw little point in false modesty. In 1819 he paused to reflect on his own brilliance:

A portrait of Metternich

1 There is a wide sweep about my mind. I am always above and
  beyond the preoccupations of most public men; I cover a ground
  much vaster than they can see, or wish to see. I cannot keep myself
  from saying about twenty times a day: how right I am and how
5 wrong they are.

In addition to vanity and arrogance there was a taste for the pomposities
of power. Metternich enjoyed nothing so much as lengthy speech, so
long as it was his. Indeed, he openly bragged about his ability to bore
people to sleep. But he was also capable of being the most frivolous of
dandies. Although it is routinely stated that he restored the Habsburgs
to their former glory at the Congress of Vienna in 1815, the fact that he
devoted most of his time at the Congress to the pursuit of various
mistresses and to his social role as a master of ceremonies is normally
overlooked. However, there were serious motives beneath the frivolity.
For Metternich politics was a social art: gossip and tittle-tattle might in
the end prove useful. It is no coincidence that he often chose to flirt with
the wives of powerful men. In 1806, for example, whilst an ambassador
in Paris, he dared to have an affair with Napoleon's sister, Caroline
Murat, in part to discover more of the French Emperor's plans.
    But his appetite for high society went far deeper than mere pleasure or
intrigue. He regarded it as part of his duties to behave as he felt a grand
aristocrat should. He consciously sought to embody the ideal of a
cultured and high-born gentleman. He loaned himself large amounts of
state money in order to surround himself with ostentatious fine arts. He
totally ignored the talk of corruption and wastefulness that this caused.
He was in politics to preserve the aristocracy, and opulence was, to his
mind, the hall-mark of true aristocracy. But there was also a darkness
lurking behind the rather forced gaiety. As he grew older he became
convinced that he was living in an age of transition. In his later writings a
distinctly pessimistic and fatalistic note comes through. In 1830 for
example he wrote that:

    my most secret conviction is that the old Europe is nearing its end.
    I have determined to fall with it, and I shall know how to do my
    duty ... my life has coincided with a most abominable time.

Despite this, Metternich kept up his various social roles - pompous
politician, amusing dandy, and the prophet of doom - to the end of his
career. It is these numerous masks that make him such an intriguing, yet
elusive, historical figure to study.

2 Historical Interpretations of Metternich

Historians have tended to judge Metternich according to the standards
and priorities of their own age. In the second half of the nineteenth

century, when the great unifications of Italy and Germany made nationalism appear triumphant, Metternich was regarded as nothing more than a failed reactionary: a man who had attempted to stand in the way of progress. The First World War gave nationalism a bad name and to a certain extent Metternich's reputation revived. In 1925 Heinrich von Srbik published a two volume biography which portrayed Metternich as a man of ideas whose profound grasp of conservative principles informed his every action. His attempt to maintain European stability through the Congress system was projected as an early attempt to construct a kind of League of Nations. After the Second World War the context changed yet again. The historiography of Metternich became dominated by scholars who had fled from Austria during the Nazi occupation and who inevitably tended to look back to the Habsburg Empire with nostalgia. In addition to this, the onset of the Cold War helped some American writers such as Henry Kissinger to see Metternich's attempt to police Europe against revolution as comparable to America's efforts to fight Communism across the globe. One suspects that the movement towards greater European unity occurring today will duly prompt someone to picture Metternich as the patron saint of a supra-national Europeanism.

However, even allowing for these trends, it is clear that historians have been more negative than positive in their assessment of Metternich. Extreme critics of Metternich such as Viktor Bibl, whose main work was produced in the 1930s, have portrayed him as an egotistical monster who would do anything to stay in power even though he knew his policies to be ultimately destructive. Bibl also argued that Metternich exploited his power for his own financial gain and that his failure to reform the Empire condemned it to eventual disintegration. In 1962 Paul Schroeder presented a more convincing portrait of Metternich as an opportunist working primarily for narrowly Austrian interests rather than for European stability. Schroeder also argued that Metternich was a poor policy maker, having few original ideas and a dogmatic commitment to the status quo which made any reform impossible.

By way of contrast, Alan Sked has gone a long way to countering most of the criticism aimed at Metternich. He has argued that Metternich sincerely believed that what was good for the Habsburg Empire would necessarily be good for Europe: that the Empire was in a sense Europe in microcosm. He has also pointed out that Metternich was not actually ruling the Empire and that he was therefore forced to work within a given framework and set of limitations. In addition, Sked has argued that even Metternich's more obviously repressive policies such as the widespread use of secret police have to be set against the background of similar practices by governments right across Europe.

Clearly historians have given us numerous Metternichs. The student's task is to test the many accounts and interpretations against the known facts in order to fashion his or her own image of the man.

3 The Metternich System

Metternich's foreign and domestic policies appear to demonstrate a large degree of common purpose: to prevent revolution or indeed any liberal or nationalist reforms and to preserve rule by monarchy and the social dominance of the aristocracy. Metternich's single-mindedness prompted contemporary commentators to speak of a 'Metternich System' and historians have subsequently found this a useful concept to help analyse his actions.

The system was applied in both foreign and domestic policy. Outside the Empire, beginning at the grand peace congress of Vienna in 1815, Metternich sought to achieve co-operation and agreement between the great powers - Russia, Prussia, Britain and the Habsburg Empire - which had combined to defeat Napoleonic France. He attempted to foster amongst them an awareness that it was in their common interest, as aristocratic powers ruled by hereditary monarchs, to avoid conflicts and to assist each other in the fight against subversives. Thus the 'Congress System' of the 1820s, involving the meeting together of representatives of the Great Powers in order to attempt to solve problems that might have led to warfare, is often seen as part of Metternich's broader system. Within the Empire, Metternich established what has been described as a police state. Using spies, censors, codebreakers, informers and the ordinary forces of law and order he sought to prevent the expression of ideas that might threaten the stability of the state.

It may seem that Metternich's system was simply a determination to snuff out reform movements wherever they appeared. However, it has been suggested by some historians that the system was more sophisticated than that, in that it was based not on naked class interest but on complex conservative philosophy. It is certainly true that Metternich's letters and memoirs offer ample evidence to show that he was ideologically committed to the *Ancien Régime* and opposed to the ideas of all reformers and revolutionaries. A few extracts from his writings will demonstrate this:

1 Two words suffice to create evil; two words which because they are devoid of any practical meaning delight the visionaries. The words are liberty and equality ... liberty of what? Liberty to do good or to do evil?
5   The people let themselves be duped easily enough: you cannot exaggerate the goodness of the people; but their ignorance is great; therefore they must be led.

And on the question of forms of government:

A king must never sacrifice any part of his authority.

Evidently Metternich was a solid, old-fashioned conservative. But some historians such as Heinrich von Srbik have argued that his system was rooted in a very complex understanding of conservative philosophy. According to von Srbik, Metternich was heavily influenced by eighteenth century dualist philosophy. Dualists argued that all life is a struggle between two opposing forces, although there was widespread disagreement among them about the nature of these forces. Metternich, according to von Srbik, came to believe that there was a struggle between destructive forces - namely nationalism, liberalism and all forms of radicalism - and the conserving force which sought to preserve the natural order of things, and that at times in history when the destructive force seemed particularly strong it was necessary to oppose it as fiercely as possible in order to attain the desired state of equilibrium or repose. Hence Metternich came to see himself as representing a necessary opposing force or counterweight. Because the theory rested on the assumption of two contending opposites, he was deeply suspicious of compromise. For him, monarchy had to be opposed to popular sovereignty and there could be no mixture of the two. The masses were to be seen as a potentially destructive force which had to be controlled. Classes, like states, must exist in a state of equilibrium, as indeed must the various ethnic groups within the Empire. In the broadest sense Metternich felt that the Empire formed the fulcrum of Europe's own balance of power.

However, some historians have been very sceptical about the idea that Metternich's actions were based upon profound philosophical beliefs. For example, A.J.P. Taylor believed that Metternich's utterances about equilibrium were nothing more than the platitudes of his class, and that 'most men could do better than this when shaving'. Between these two extremes, Sked has argued that what Metternich described as his 'boring old principles' consisted of respect for treaties and for the rule of law more generally, in addition to a belief in co-operation and consultation between the great powers.

So was there a Metternich system? Before attempting an answer to that question it is important to look at Metternich's actions both at home and abroad.

4 The Metternich System in Domestic Policy

Did Metternich dominate and control the Habsburg Empire? This is the basic question lurking behind any assessment of a domestic Metternich system. But this question is rather more complex than it seems. In order to tackle it with as much clarity as possible it is helpful to sub-divide the problem into three separate aspects. Firstly, there is a need to look at perhaps the most stereotypical image of Metternich's control, the so-called 'police state' and the question of how far he was able to control the flow of revolutionary ideas within the Empire. However, there is also a need to look beyond Metternich's use of police at the broader question of how effectively he actually dealt with specific reform or revolutionary movements. For this reason a second section has been devoted to an examination of Metternich's handling of the most pressing internal threats to the Empire: Magyar and Italian nationalism. Thirdly, there is the question of exactly how much political power Metternich enjoyed. The idea that he imposed a systematic control over the Habsburg Empire presupposes that he had almost unlimited political influence. But how far was that actually the case? Having examined these three facets of the problem it ought then to be possible to make an informed judgement about the extent of Metterich's control.

a) Metternich and the Police State

In support of the idea that Metternich was able to control the political life of the Empire is the commonly asserted notion that he turned the Empire into a 'police state' in which all revolutionary ideas were effectively suppressed. How much truth is there in this view?

The police force was run by a separate ministry headed by a Director. Between 1816 and 1848 the Director was Count Sedlnitzky - a man appointed by Emperor Francis I for his ceaseless flattery - who came to form a powerful loyalty to Metternich. The two men worked very closely together and as a result Metternich came to know more about what was going on in the Empire than the Emperor.

The police department was responsible not only for the maintenance of law and order throughout the Empire but also for the enforcement of a strict censorship and a broad surveillance of the activities and opinions of all subjects. The uniformed official police formed a network of law enforcing officers that stretched right across the Empire. Their main tasks were to maintain law and order and to ensure that all subjects were registered with the state bureaucracy. In practice their effectiveness depended on the degree of co-operation they could obtain from the local governors and the leading nobles in the area because the police force was surprisingly small in number. In Vienna, for example, before 1848 the regular force consisted of 7 officers, 78 NCOs and 490 men. There was also a small mounted force and a civilian guard, but clearly these numbers were inadequate for controlling any kind of major revolt in a city with a population of 400,000. Therefore to talk of a police state in the sense that the people were intimidated by a police presence in large numbers is quite wrong.

However, much more central to any notion of a police state is the question of Metternich's use of a secret police. There can be no doubt that he did employ not only a secret police force but also a shady collection of unofficial spies and informers to probe into almost any aspect of the lives of the people. Their first duty was to keep watch on suspicious individuals, particularly liberals, nationalists and radical students and their professors. In order to do this they opened the mail of anybody and everybody, and they censored plays, poems, novels, and newspapers. Even the less obviously political aspects of communication such as paintings and music were subject to rigorous scrutiny.

The ideas of nationalists and liberals were to be excluded from the Empire. It was also the task of the secret police to prevent any religious works entering the country which represented a threat to Catholic orthodoxy. Jewish works were particularly abhorrent and were frequently banned. There was, in short, no area of the Empire's cultural or ideological life that the censors and spies would not touch. For example, in 1824, the secret police devoted time and money to the surveillance of Italians wearing a certain sort if tie pin on the false suspicion that this may have been the covert insignia of a secret nationalist masonic lodge.

Of particular concern to Metternich and his Director of Police was the threat of subversive liberal or nationalist ideas coming into the Empire from abroad. Metternich sought, through censorship imposed within the Post Office and through the editing of foreign news items, to seal off Austria from the reality of what was happening in the rest of Europe. The Press was used to create a fictional Europe in which all events and ideas reinforced the rightness of the existing system in the Empire. The methods were not as unsubtle as perhaps they sound. Metternich shrewdly employed some of the Empire's most talented writers to produce the kind of copy that was not overtly propagandist. It was more a celebration of the charms of life in such a civilised Imperial state.

At its most sinister the system could sanction random house searches and even arrest without specific charges. Occasionally people simply disappeared for lengthy periods before finally coming to trial on trumped-up charges. Suspected political agitators were particularly vulnerable to such arbitrary practices. It is this shadowy world of secret police, spies and censors that was the reality of any Metternich system.

But how effective was this supposed system? In might be seen as remarkably effective given that between 1815 and 1847 there was no serious revolutionary threat within the Empire. And yet imposing ideological uniformity in such a vast Empire was an astonishingly difficult task. Metternich may have been quite successful in muzzling the domestic press but he found it almost impossible to prevent subversive foreign literature entering the country. It seems that those people who sought subversive literature had little difficulty in finding it. Indeed it appears that the authorities and the people they sought to coerce evolved a cosy conspiracy in which it was recognised both that nobody should read dissident literature and that all educated men did. So long as no one actually wanted to act upon these dangerous principles in a way that might harm the Empire then few questions were asked.

Given this laxity it has to be wondered whether the term 'police state' is still appropriate. After all, it is a label most associated with such brutal regimes as Nazi Germany and Stalinist Russia. Metternich's Austria was not nearly so chillingly efficient or so violent as these notorious examples. Metternich did not have suspects murdered or tortured: the prisons were not brimming over with political prisoners.

Nevertheless, the subjects of the Habsburg Empire must have frequently felt the presence of the state snooping on their lives. But the police state was not a brutal tyranny nor even an efficient apparatus of state control. If it was a police state it was a police state of its time and almost quaint in its incompetence in comparison with subsequent totalitarian regimes.

b) Internal Threats to the Empire

i) Metternich and Magyar Nationalism

Nineteenth-century Magyar nationalism, like so many of the nationalist movements of that century, had its roots in the Napoleonic period. Where it perhaps differed from the nationalism of western Europe was in the social background of its main proponents. Magyar nationalism was very largely restricted to the land-owning classes - the upper nobility and the gentry. The middle classes were too few in number in Hungary to be politically significant and the peasantry were preoccupied with day-to-day subsistence.

The wars against Napoleon indirectly helped to fuel a nationalist movement in Hungary amongst the nobles for two main reasons. Firstly, the cost of the war brought Francis I into conflict with the Hungarian Diet. In 1812 he asked for a large war subsidy to be granted and the Diet refused to agree to it. In response Francis prorogued the parliament and ruled Hungary by decree for the next thirteen years. During these years the resentment of the nobility increased considerably. Secondly, war took many of the nobility into western Europe for the first time. As a result, the nobility became aware that western Europe enjoyed a higher standard of living than in the east. Some of the nobility therefore returned to Hungary to demand political and economic change. For Metternich the very notion of change was tantamount to a call for revolution.

Within the emerging Magyar nationalist movement there were two recognisably different strands - moderates and radicals or, as Metternich liked to call them, the 'old opposition' of the aristocracy and the 'lunatic opposition' of the gentry. However, although he recognised the distinction, he rejected the claims of both groups. The moderates were led by Count Széchényi, an aristocrat from one of the leading families in Hungary. His pedigree was unquestionable and his family took pride in a long tradition of loyal service to the Habsburg crown. But there was also a pride in their Magyar identity. Indeed Széchényi's father set up

Hungary's first National Library. Széchényi saw no conflict between his reform programme and loyalty to the Habsburgs. In essence his ideas were economic rather than political. As a result of his travels with the Habsburg armies in the Napoleonic wars and of his post-war trip to England, he became a convinced westerniser. He argued strongly that Hungarian agriculture must seek to learn from the improvements made in the west. He called for the abolition of serfdom and a transition to a capitalist agriculture based on wage labour. This, he argued, was in the interest of the nobility as they would eventually become wealthier. Széchényi was, like many other nobles, in chronic debt and his envisaged agricultural revolution was undoubtedly designed, in part, to solve the problems facing the nobility as a class. However, Széchényi expected that it would also generate improvements for all other Hungarians. The abolition of serfdom would allow far greater social mobility and an improved education system would help to create the so-called 'career open to the talents'. Although Széchényi preached loyalty to the Habsburgs, Metternich did not look upon his policies favourably.

Indeed, Széchényi was only once successful in persuading the chancellor to adopt one of his ideas for Hungary and it is at least arguable that this happened because Metternich was too busy with foreign policy to pay proper attention to Hungarian issues. In 1830 when Metternich was preoccupied with the revolution in France, Széchényi managed to persuade Francis I that Hungarian ought to be the recognised language of officialdom and of parliamentary record rather than Latin. After 1836 Hungarian became the language of officialdom throughout Hungary and began to be taught in schools far more effectively and rigorously than had been the case before. The linguistic triumph undoubtedly gave a great boost to the nationalist cause as nationalist teachers began to unearth histories of Hungary or classics of Hungarian literature and to inspire their young students with a sense of Hungary's past and potential future greatness.

Ironically, Széchényi came to doubt the wisdom of these changes. This first stage in what historians tend to call 'Magyarisation' profoundly alienated the other ethnic groups living in this sector of the empire. The Croats were particularly resentful and nursed a growing hatred of the Magyars. The Habsburgs found themselves in a dilemma that would become more familiar - concessions for the sake of stability would provoke new causes of instability.

It was this 'Catch-22' logic that led Metternich to oppose Széchényi's ideas for reform even though they were very moderate. He was forced to give way on the language question because Francis overruled him, but he was successful in his opposition to almost every other aspect of Széchényi's programme. In order to achieve this he fostered links with reliable conservative politicians such as Count Apponyi, the Hungarian chancellor, and used this connection to mobilise opinion in the

Hungarian Diet against Széchényi. When Széchényi eventually managed to put his case for economic reforms to Metternich in person he was rudely fobbed off with the observation that if you 'take one stone out of the vaulting, the whole thing collapses'.

Metternich's commitment to this principle was quite unswerving and no concessions were given. As a result, it was Széchényi who collapsed. His frustration with Metternich, with his own class, with the lack of interest shown by foreign capitalists and with what he regarded as the extremism coming from the gentry literally drove him mad. He ended his days in an asylum in Vienna where he eventually committed suicide.

The unofficial leader of the radical nationalist movement in the 1830s and 1840s was Louis Kossuth. Széchényi regarded Kossuth as a dangerous extremist, whilst Kossuth regarded the grand aristocrat as a fawning lackey to the Habsburgs. Kossuth is best described as both a nationalist and a liberal. His nationalism led him to call for a Hungarian parliament with complete power to rule over Hungarian affairs without interference from Vienna. He was very much in favour of the Magyarisation of the nation's life. He applauded the legal changes which made Magyar the official language and seemed apparently unconcerned about the resentment this provoked amongst the various other ethnic groups, such as the Croats and the Romanians, within Hungarian territories.

His liberalism was consciously modelled on liberalism as it had been defined in western Europe. He demanded a free press, trial by jury, penal reform and parliamentary government. But in one respect he was distinctly out of step with western European liberalism. He was not in favour of free trade. His recipe for economic reform in Hungary was not that different to Széchényi's, except that he wanted tariff protection for Hungarian produce. His particular concern was to obtain protection for Hungary from economic exploitation by Austria. Kossuth argued that Hungary had been forced into a kind of colonial relationship with the more advanced sectors of the Empire. The only way that Hungarian industry could thrive would be if the goods produced elsewhere in the Empire had tariffs imposed upon them when they entered Hungary. If this were done Hungary might eventually be able to compete on equal terms.

As a result of printing such ideas, Kossuth was thrown into prison in 1837 for three years. On his release he found himself to be a national hero, especially among that section of the declining nobility which blamed its woes on Vienna. Out of prison, he became editor of *Pesti Hirlap* (the *Pest Herald* newspaper) and dramatically built up its readership by preaching a romantic message of radical nationalism. His calls for the abolition of serfdom and more democracy gave him a broad base of popular support. In 1847 he was elected to the Lower House of the Hungarian Diet. On the eve of the 1848 revolutions Kossuth was the obvious focus of any revolutionary nationalist movement.

How effectively had Metternich dealt with the threat posed by Hungarian nationalism? It seems evident that his only clear policy was complete rejection of any reforms. His total rejection of Széchényi's moderate-loyalist nationalism was surely a mistake because it only served to drive moderate nationalists into the Kossuth camp. His approach to Kossuth seems equally unproductive. The attempt to suppress him by sending him to prison had precisely the reverse effect. Prison was the making of Kossuth, giving him the necessary credentials as a martyr to the cause. It seems fair to argue that the Metternich system was a system almost bound to self-destruct. It is therefore fitting that on 3 March 1848 it was Kossuth's speech which ignited the Hungarian revolution which led to the collapse of the policy and the exile of its author.

ii) Metternich and Italian Nationalism

Metternich regarded the entire Italian peninsula exactly as he regarded Germany, as an area to be controlled, either directly or indirectly, by the Habsburgs. In 1805 Napoleon had taken most of the Habsburg possessions in Italy but Metternich had reasserted Austrian domination in the peace settlement of 1815. After 1815 Francis I was appointed as ruler of the kingdom of Lombardy-Venetia. This was the only part of the peninsula over which the Habsburgs ruled directly but Francis's control of the north was reinforced by the fact that his brother was Grand Duke of Tuscany, his daughter reigned in Parma and his cousin ruled over Modena. The remaining northern Italian state, Piedmont, posed no threat until the circumstances created by the revolutions of 1848 encouraged its king to make a bid for Lombardy-Venetia.

Central Italy was still in the possession of the papacy, but in the years after 1815 the Church was deeply sympathetic to Metternich's conservative aims. As a result, the Habsburgs were able to negotiate the right to station troops in papal territory. Not until the accession of Pope Pius IX in 1846 did the Habsburgs have any worries about Rome as an ally in the struggle against Italian nationalism. Pope Pius IX was that most unusual of creatures, a liberal Pope - or at least he thought he was until the revolutions of 1848 changed his mind for him. Nevertheless the accession of a progressive Pope gave a boost to Italian nationalists and in some ways helped to foment the upheavals of 1848.

In the south of the peninsula Naples and Sicily were controlled by the Bourbon King Ferdinand who was loyal to the Habsburgs, mainly as a result of his memories of exile during the Napoleonic period which left him with a terror of revolution. He was also married to a Habsburg.

Clearly, the 1815 settlement left the Habsburgs as the dominant power in Italy. For better or worse Metternich had pitted the Empire against Italian nationalism. But he did not see this as a mistake. He sincerely believed that Italy was merely a 'geographical expression'. His view was that Italian nationalism was restricted to a handful of extremists and that it was something deliberately fuelled by the French as part of their territorial ambitions in the region. Thus Metternich had two aims in Italy - to suppress the nationalists and to keep France out. He took great pride in the fact that there was far less nationalist agitation in Lombardy-Venetia than elsewhere in the peninsula. He believed that this was due less to what he called 'enlightened administration' than to the large military and police presence and the network of spies that operated.

Although the Habsburgs did set up resident viceroys as the living symbols of Habsburg authority in Italy, all the important decisions regarding Lombardy-Venetia were made in Vienna. Metternich approved of this centralised rule but he grew increasingly frustrated with the slowness of the decision-making process. The Imperial bureaucracy in conjunction with the Council of State were responsible for making the policy - a task that was in itself lengthy - and then Francis would have to approve it.

However, Metternich regarded Italy as his legitimate sphere of influence and he rapidly found ways of asserting his own control in Lombardy-Venetia. In 1826 he sent a special agent to Milan in order to organise an information network which would relay information directly back to him. In a sense he short-circuited the bureaucracy out of the system of rule. His direct control of the army meant that he could rapidly act upon information received and arrest anybody suspected of nationalist activities. As elsewhere in the Empire, Metternich imposed rigid censorship. Italians were not allowed to read anything which might remotely stimulate patriotic feelings. Classic Italian literature was banned and only Austrian history was taught in the schools.

In addition to these coercive measures, Metternich sought to kill Italian nationalism with kindness. Habsburg rule in north Italy could not be described as harsh or tyrannical; indeed Metternich never ceased to point out that Italian subjects of the Habsburgs enjoyed equality before the law, reasonably low levels of taxation and a standard of living that compared favourably with their fellow Italians outside of the Empire.

However, this combination of coercion and kindness was not successful in eliminating Italian nationalism. Metternich could police the nationalists in Lombardy-Venetia but he had less control of them elsewhere in the peninsula. In the south, secret societies such as the Carbonari sprang up, and amongst the middle classes a movement known as Young Italy sought, quite successfully, to promote a national consciousness amongst all Italians.

However, although Metternich could not hope to impose ideological control over all of Italy, he was remarkably successful in his attempts to persuade other Italian powers to help suppress any nationalist revolts on the peninsula. In 1821 he was faced with a rebellion in Naples which was more liberal than nationalist. However, had it been successful it would have set a dangerous example that might have been followed in other Italian states. To complicate matters, the French were backing the rebel calls for some sort of constitutional monarchy, apparently with the support of Tsar Alexander I. Metternich called a special Congress at Troppau to discuss the situation and used the forum to present the Naples rebellion as a threat to the entire European order established at the Congress of Vienna. His argument convinced the Tsar and so Metternich was able to send Austrian troops into Naples to crush the rising and to present his actions to the world as the work of the Congress or Alliance system - he was too diplomatic to refer to it as the Metternich system! Also in 1821 Austrian troops suppressed a rising in Piedmont and re-established a legitimate, absolutist monarch. Then, in 1831, Metternich sent troops into Modena, Parma and the Papal States to quell liberal and nationalist uprisings. Evidently he was able to police the peninsula very effectively. Italian nationalists in Lombardy-Venetia never seriously threatened Habsburg rule. Further south Austrian military force consistently frustrated the liberals and the nationalists.

But the story is not entirely one of success. As his arch rival at court, Count Kolowrat, never tired of pointing out, the task of patrolling all Italy was extremely costly and was dragging the crown closer and closer to bankruptcy. In addition, it seems that Metternich seriously underestimated the power of nationalism. Although he defeated it time and again, it always rose up again. It is tempting to say that the revolutions of 1848 in Italy prove that the Metternich system did not work. But this is highly debatable. Perhaps Metternich's methods fomented revolution or perhaps nationalism was simply an unstoppable force. It seems most likely that the Metternich system worked perfectly well in Italy and that it was the fall of Metternich, itself caused by other factors, which not surprisingly encouraged the Italian nationalists to rise up in 1848.

c) The Limits of Metternich's Power

Was there a recognisable Metternich system at work in the governing of the Empire? Given that Metternich's policies could be, and sometimes were, overruled by the Emperor Francis I, it is tempting to argue that there never could have been a domestic Metternich system. In addition, Metternich's famous quip that he had 'governed Europe sometimes but Austria never' could be seen as a frank recognition of the fact that almost all power in the Habsburg system of government was vested in the person of the Emperor, and that this was as he thought it ought to be, for he was a staunch defender of absolutism.

But it is clear that Metternich was deeply frustrated by what he saw as the inefficiencies and irrationalities in the Habsburg system of government. It is perhaps a little ironic that he compared the Habsburg administration unfavourably with the old Napoleonic Empire. In particular, he admired Napoleon's use of a small hand-picked Council of State as the key advisory body. In contrast, Francis had a Council of State that had evolved into a large, unwieldy body consisting of numerous unco-ordinated sections and sub-sections. In addition to this, Francis could also turn to his army of imperial civil servants for yet more advice. There was no means for the leading ministers of the crown to operate as one body. Everything depended upon the Emperor and upon whom he happened to turn to at any given moment. This created a governing machinery that was very slow moving. It was made more so by Francis's fondness for commissioning detailed reports on issues before acting.

Given the enormous power of the Emperor and the way in which the entire governmental system revolved around him, it may seem a little inappropriate to talk of Metternich's system of government. But there are reasons for believing that Metternich was able to govern from behind the throne. His relationship with Francis was very strong and the two men shared a very similar political outlook. Francis came to trust Metternich's judgement more than any other single individual's and thus Metternich was able to dominate government very effectively for most of the time until Francis's death in 1835.

Francis I was succeeded by Ferdinand I (1835-48), a well-intentioned young man who nevertheless rapidly earned for himself the soubriquet 'Ferd the Loon'. The new Emperor was extremely slow witted and prone to fits as a result of his epilepsy. The Emperor's poor mental health had profound consequences for Metternich, who quickly discovered that he could no longer subtly persuade and coax the Emperor to follow his chancellor's advice, because the Emperor could not understand it. Naturally, this had serious consequences for Metternich's position. Over the years Metternich had made enemies at court, and his inability to manipulate the new Emperor was seen by his rivals as a chance for them to break Metternich's grip on power. His main rival was the finance minister Count Kolowrat.

To a certain extent Kolowrat was motivated by a combination of resentment of Metternich's power and his own personal ambition. But he also had principled objections to Metternich's policies. Kolowrat, as finance minister, felt that only by balancing the books and ensuring the economic health of the crown could its survival be ensured. He therefore disapproved strongly of Metternich's expensive commitment to maintaining a large standing army. In 1847 Kolowrat explained to the most important of governmental committees, the Permanent Inner Conference, the extent of the crisis facing the state:

1 I feel it is my duty to make the grave statement that we are on the verge of an abyss, and the increasing demands on the Treasury arising out of the measures necessary to combat foreign revolutionary elements have led to increased disturbances within
5 the country.

Kolowrat's criticism are clearly an indictment of Metternich's expensive foreign policy and therefore also an indictment of the Metternich system. Undoubtedly Metternich had made the already dire financial position of the crown much worse. The Monarchy had declared itself bankrupt in 1811 and had been forced to borrow money thereafter at crippling interest rates. Between 1815 and 1848 interest payments accounted for 30 per cent of state revenue. In addition to this, Metternich's heavy commitment to what Kolowrat called a 'forest of bayonets' meant that the military budget accounted for a further 40 per cent of state revenues. It is clear from these figures that Metternich simply was not in a position to commit the Habsburg armies to frequent interventions around Europe as the Metternich system seemed to demand. The role he had designed for the Empire in 1815, as the policeman of Europe, was a role that thirty years later the Empire could no longer afford to play.

Kolowrat, as the man who had to find a way to pay for any wars, was made extremely nervous by Metternich's unwillingness to face financial facts. It also seems that there was an element of personal dislike and mutual suspicion between the two men. One of Kolowrat's letters sums up his feelings:

> the intolerable vanity of the man, who in all his life has never been wrong, who has always foreseen everything - and still foresees everything - that happened and that did not happen. To put it briefly, I just cannot get on with him.

Given Kolowrat's personal and principled hostility to Metternich, it is hardly surprising that he sought to exploit the power vacuum created by Francis's death to bring down the chancellor. Metternich was not unaware of the threat posed by Kolowrat. He prepared for the succession crisis by persuading the dying Francis to draft a final testament which urged Ferdinand to rely most heavily on Metternich for all decisions. However, Metternich's plans were frustrated by the intervention of Francis's three brothers, the Archdukes Ludwig, John and Charles. These men had long resented Metternich's all pervasive influence and sought to find a way to curb his power. In conjunction with Kolowrat they forced upon Ferdinand the setting up of a Regency Council consisting of themselves, Kolowrat and Metternich. The cards were now stacked heavily against Metternich.

When the revolutions broke out in 1848 Kolowrat exploited Metternich's weak position on the Regency Council in order to force his resignation. Indeed, it could be argued that it was not the revolution which toppled Metternich but a combination of Ferdinand's idiocy and Kolowrat's cunning.

5 The Metternich System in Foreign Policy

a) Metternich and Napoleon, 1809-15

For the Habsburg Empire the French Revolution and the Naploeonic Wars had been a traumatic experience. From 1792 to 1815 the Austrians were frequently at war with France. The outcomes of these wars, with the exception of the final victory, ranged from the disappointing to the disastrous.

By 1809 Napoleon had substantially reduced the size of the Empire: the Habsburgs were forced out of northern Italy, the Austrian Netherlands were placed under French control, Habsburg territory in Poland was absorbed into Napoleon's Grand Duchy of Warsaw, and even as far south-east as the Dalmatian coast, Napoleon robbed the Habsburgs in order to set up his Illyrian Kingdom. In addition to this, Napoleon dissolved the Holy Roman Empire, the traditional seat of Habsburg power over central Germany and set up his Confederation of the Rhine, thus ending 400 years of Habsburg imperial sway over German affairs. Indeed, by 1809 Napoleon was in a position to dismember the entire Empire.

It was at this crisis point that the Habsburg Emperor, Francis I, chose to appoint Metternich as foreign minister. Not surprisingly, Metternich's short-term political aim was simply to preserve the Empire. He never forgot this brush with political extinction. He worked all the rest of his ministerial life to ensure that such a moment never occurred again. This experience undoubtedly shaped all his subsequent thinking. It was also the root cause of his subsequent paranoia about France and revolution.

Metternich's astonishing achievement in the period 1809-15 was to steer this militarily and financially weakened state through a time of great danger and eventually to achieve a peace settlement which not only restored the Empire to its former grandeur but, some would say, improved upon its previous position.

However, the foreign policies he adopted to achieve these ends were markedly different from the 'system' with which he is usually associated after 1815.

His initial response to the danger was to urge Francis to ally with Napoleon. Astonishingly, Metternich also recommended to Francis that he allow his elder daughter, Marie Louise, to marry Napoleon in order to bind the new alliance. Eventually he managed to persuade a reluctant Francis that his daughter was the necessary price to be paid for the survival of the Empire and the marriage duly took place in 1810.

But, by 1812 the alliance with France had begun to look like something of an embarrassment. Austria was now not only allied to Napoleon but allied to a Napoleon who seemed likely to lose. Metternich now perceived a new threat: a peace settlement dictated by the Russian Tsar Alexander I. The Tsar was known to have designs on former Habsburg territories in Poland. In February 1813 the Tsar formed an alliance with Prussia, the Treaty of Kalisch, in which the Prussians agreed to allow Russians a free hand in Poland if they would further Prussian ambitions in Germany. This was a threat to Habsburg pre-eminence in Germany. This twin threat to Habsburg interests in Poland and Germany, both areas of former Habsburg influence, was to dominate Metternich's approach to the final stages of the war.

Metternich hoped that Napoleon and his Habsburg wife would arrive at a negotiated peace and that he might therefore be able to use the French alliance against Russia. However, when it became clear that Napoleon was not going to compromise Metternich altered his approach to the Russian problem. In August 1813, in something of a diplomatic *volte-face,* he threw Austria's weight into the coalition against Napoleon. He gradually came to believe that the only way to restrain Russian and therefore Prussian influence was through his personal diplomacy. As the Napoleonic wars drew to a close all the great powers began to consider how best they could ensure their respective share of the spoils. Metternich put his faith in the idea of a grand peace congress. One of his greatest political talents was his persuasiveness. A congress would give him the ideal opportunity to exploit his political charms, subtly to cajole and manipulate a peace settlement in the Habsburg interest.

He had already established an important precedent for this mode of conducting international relations when in 1814 he had engineered a congress of the four great powers known as the Congress of Chatillon. This led to the Treaty of Chaumont in which the great powers agreed to remain allied for the next twenty years against any threat from France. They also agreed to meet collectively in the event of crises. Thus even before Napoleon was finally defeated Metternich had established the idea of co-operation between the great powers which was so fundamental to the post-war Metternich system. After the defeat of Napoleon he persuaded the allies that not only should a grand peace congress be called but that it should be held in Vienna. The Congress of Vienna which opened in November 1814 not only marked the end of the Napoleonic era but it also ushered in, though few realised it at the time, the Age of Metternich.

b) The Congress of Vienna

The Congress at Vienna was an impressive event. It attracted not only the heads of state of all the major powers, with the exception of the intermittently insane George III, but also the heads of most of Europe's greatest aristocratic families and their wives. Metternich made every effort to ensure that the occasion was as enjoyable as possible, setting up a Festivals Committee to lay on numerous balls and masked entertainments. Such was his commitment to pleasure that one observer complained that he had become 'intolerably loose and giddy with women'. Tsar Alexander I grew extremely annoyed with the Austrian foreign minister's endless flirtations, although it seems this feeling was also tinged with a certain amount of jealousy. And, of course, Metternich's lightheartedness was to some extent another mask behind which to hide while he contemplated the serious business of securing a peace settlement that was both favourable to the Habsburgs and acceptable to the other great powers.

Although the Congress had many issues to resolve, there were two that stood out as likely to lead to conflict between Austria and Russia. These were the Polish and the German questions. The Tsar hoped to call upon Prussian support for his aim of creating a Polish kingdom entirely under Russian rule. In return he would ensure that Prussia acquired all of Saxony. This would be a double blow to Habsburg interests. In particular Metternich sought to regain Habsburg control of Germany. In order to achieve this Metternich indulged in a little behind-the-scenes touting for support. He had already won over the English foreign secretary, Castlereagh, to his way of thinking before the Congress met by informing him that the Tsar wanted to put his own candidate on the French throne. Metternich and Castlereagh were agreed that only a restoration of the Bourbons would be acceptable. It also seems that Castlereagh shared a suspicion of Russia. Metternich was therefore able to persuade Castlereagh that Austria ought to be supported against Russian expansion.

Metternich's masterstroke at Vienna was to persuade the other powers, with the support of Castlereagh, to allow the French a say in the negotiations. This was important because thereby the French foreign minister, Talleyrand, was allowed a vote, and Metternich had already made sure of his support for Austria against Russia. As Metternich understood, Talleyrand was happy to agree to anything that would end France's diplomatic isolation. Thus with British and French support Metternich was able to force a settlement to the Polish-Saxon problem which suited the Habsburgs. In Poland the Tsar got his kingdom but Austria retained a sizeable slice of Polish territory in Galicia. More importantly, in Germany it was agreed that a 39-state German Confederation would be set up with a diet at Frankfurt and that the Habsburgs would occupy the presidency of this new German parliament. Thus Metternich achieved a major objective: the restoration of Habsburg control over Germany. In fact, her domination of Germany was now more effective than it had been in the last days of the Holy Roman Empire. Prussia had to be content with two-fifths of Saxon territory, but was compensated with a sizeable amount of the industrially expanding Rhineland, as well as Pomerania. The acquisition of the Rhineland was highly significant in the long term because of the economic power it conferred on Prussia, but Metternich could not have been expected to recognise this at the time.

Once these questions were out of the way it was relatively easy for Metternich to achieve his other main aim - the restoration of Habsburg domination in northern Italy. The allies recognised the legality of the Austrian seizure of Lombardy and Venetia that had already taken place. Both Metternich and the Emperor placed a high priority on reasserting Habsburg influence in Italian affairs. The fact that the Emperor's daughter was granted the key northern duchies of Parma, Piacenza and Guastalla further guaranteed Habsburg sway over northern Italy.

In addition to Germany and Italy, Metternich tied up a number of other loose ends, retaking the south Slav lands along the Dalmatian coastline and adding some relatively new territories such as the Duchy of Salzburg which had been independent before the wars with France began. There is no doubt that, from the Habsburg point of view, Metternich's performance at Vienna was a remarkable personal *tour de force*.

c) Defending the Vienna Settlement

What made the Vienna settlement such an astonishing and durable settlement was that it had been achieved without seriously alienating any of the great powers. Even the Tsar left Vienna reasonably satisfied with his gains, although with the faint suspicion that he had not been accorded sufficient respect by the superficially charming Austrian minister.

Once Metternich had performed the miracle of reconstructing an Empire that only six years before had seemed about to disintegrate he became obsessed with the idea of defending this settlement. However, he realised that Austria was too weak to defend the Vienna settlement on her own. Only through collective action could the restored *Ancien Régime* protect itself against any further French-style revolutions. But Metternich was not alone in thinking this way. The belief in collective action in order to preserve the settlement was shared at first by the three other major powers - Russia, Prussia and Britain. In November 1815 - after the alliance had been put to the trouble of defeating Napoleon for a second time following his flight from Elba - the four states agreed to remain allied for the next twenty years in order to defend the Vienna settlement against any renewed threat from France. Thus was born the so-called Quadruple Alliance.

The allies also agreed on a method for dealing with trouble as it arose. They decided that in the event of an uprising in Europe the great powers would call a congress to decide upon united action. This has become known as the Congress System. To try to avoid confusion it is probably best to think of the Congress System as a sub-system within Metternich's broader ideological system - a diplomatic means to a Metternichian end.

However, there was also considerable rivalry between the so-called allies. Tsar Alexander I was determined to impose his ideas upon the other allies. To this end, also in 1815, he constructed another alliance known as the Holy Alliance. The Tsar's alliance was intended to be an aggressively Christian league prepared to intervene anywhere in Europe where liberals, nationalists or any other sort of dissident caused trouble. The Holy Allies pledged themselves, in theory at least, to police Europe against liberalism and nationalism, even if this meant intervening in the domestic affairs of other countries. Metternich persuaded the Austrian Emperor to sign his name to it, though he privately dismissed it as a 'loud sounding nothing'. There was no point in offending the Tsar. The King of Prussia, along with virtually every European ruler, also signed. The major exception was George III. The British government refused to commit itself to the alliance, arguing that no one should meddle in the purely domestic affairs of a sovereign nation.

Already it was clear that Metternich's ideal of a concert between the four great powers which had defeated Napoleon was likely to be torn apart by the very different attitudes and aims of the protagonists. A liberal constitutional monarchy like Britain was unlikely to share the same outlook as the large absolutist states of Eastern Europe. So the argument that Metternich orchestrated the four great powers to play the same reactionary tune is not tenable. However, he did play a key role in restraining the Russians and reassuring the British.

For several years after the Congress of Vienna the four great powers did respond to crises in Europe by calling further congresses. To begin with the fact that there existed two rather contradictory sets of alliances seemed not to matter. Between 1815 and 1820 the Congress system appeared to work. But gradually the ideological differences existing between the great powers rendered four power co-operation impossible.

i) The Revolutions of 1820-1 and the End of the Congress System

The first major threat to the new order came in 1820 with revolutions beginning in Naples, Piedmont, and Spain. At the Congress of Troppau Metternich persuaded the allies that Austrian forces ought to intervene in Italy. This they did, successfully restoring absolute monarchy in both Naples and Piedmont. However, Castlereagh, Britain's foreign minister, made it extremely clear in the famous state paper of 5 May 1820 that Britain did not endorse the principle of intervention in the internal affairs of other nations. The Congress system and indeed the entire Quadruple Alliance began to look extremely fragile.

Metternich was extremely worried that the withdrawal of Britain from the alliance would make it all the easier for Alexander I to dominate the policies of the remaining allies. The first hint of problems to come for Metternich was the Tsar's determination to back French intervention in Spain where a revolt threatened to bring down Ferdinand VII.

Metternich argued that it was contrary to the principles of the

Quadruple Alliance to back a French invasion of another country. He retained a profound suspicion of French expansionism. In his view to back French action in Spain would be to go directly against the spirit of the Congress of Vienna. He felt sure that with Castlereagh's support the alliance could be steered to oppose France. Unfortunately for him Castlereagh committed suicide by slitting his throat with a pen knife just before the critical Congress of Verona when the whole issue was to be discussed. By taking his life when he did, Castlereagh had also unwittingly killed the Congress System. George Canning, his replacement as foreign minister, was a liberal in foreign policy and refused even to attend the Congress. As a result, the Tsar, with the aid of Prussia, steamrollered Metternich into following Russia's line. With Britain now explicitly out of the alliance, Russia was in a position to dominate any future congress. Therefore, it is surely no coincidence that after 1822 Metternich neither proposed nor attended any more great power congresses.

After the breakdown of the Congress System Russia and Austria increasingly vied for domination of the alliance. The two main allies began to appear increasingly as rivals. Indeed, the nationalist revolt occurring in Greece from 1821 onwards threatened to destroy the alliance altogether.

Metternich saw the Greek revolt against Ottoman rule as another clear case of a nationalist threat to legitimate monarchy. However, the Tsar was in something of a dilemma. Although he also detested the spectacle of a nationalist revolt, the Greek rebels were fellow members of the Orthodox church and for that reason, in the Tsar's eyes, deserved support against the infidel Turk. But Metternich suspected that the Tsar had a hidden agenda - to weaken the Ottoman Empire in the Balkans so that Russia might extend her influence there.

At first Metternich managed to persuade the Tsar not to intervene on behalf of the Greeks and thus saved the Holy Alliance. However, when Alexander I died in 1825 he was succeeded by his brother Nicholas I who was determined to take stronger action. By 1828 Russia was at war with the Turks. Metternich was appalled. In 1830 the Turks finally agreed to the setting up of an independent Greek state and Russia backed away from the possibility of bringing about the complete collapse of the Ottoman Empire for fear of the unpredictable consequences. Metternich heaved a sigh of relief. However, the Holy Alliance was in tatters. Furthermore, the weakness of the Ottoman Empire seemed to make further tension between Austria and Russia inevitable.

But events conspired to resolve the problem. The wave of revolutions that broke out in Europe in 1830 dramatically changed Tsar Nicholas's attitude to revolt, and in 1833 he came to Metternich, in his own words, 'as a pupil to a master' to forge an agreement over the Turkish question. The result was the Münchengrätz Agreement in which the Tsar and Metternich agreed to maintain the Ottoman Empire and only to act after consultation should dismemberment become unavoidable. This was an exceptionally effective piece of diplomacy which enabled Austria to feel secure in the east whilst simultaneously resurrecting the spirit of the Holy Alliance.

ii) Metternich and the German Confederation

Metternich regarded German territory exactly as he tended to regard Italian territory - as part of the Habsburg's unofficial Empire. Although Napoleon had succeeded in abolishing the Holy Roman Empire which had for so long been the means by which the Habsburgs controlled Germany, the creation of the German Confederation at the Congress of Vienna in 1815 enabled the Habsburgs to reassert themselves in Germany even more forcibly than before. The constitution of the Confederation allowed for the permanent Habsburg presidency, and thus the Diet which met at Frankfurt, although attended by representatives of the other 38 states, was in fact simply the mechanism for maintaining Habsburg hegemony in Germany.

However, there were a number of possible threats to the continuation of Habsburg domination. The most obvious challenges came from the liberals and the nationalists. The liberals wanted a shift towards constitutional monarchy and the nationalists hoped to find some means of promoting eventual German unification. In both cases the people who made up these groups tended to be young students from the disaffected middle classes and their teachers. Metternich monitored the activities of all student groups as closely as he could through his network of spies. In 1819 a revolutionary student assassinated an agent of the Tsar, and Metternich seized the opportunity to pass legislation against potential dissidents. The Karlsbad Decrees allowed the authorities to arrest any teachers suspected of subversive activities and to disband student societies. In some cases whole universities were closed down. A commission was set up to maintain surveillance on students and a law was passed to allow the Confederation to censor or ban any newspaper or pamphlet. However, this was insufficient to solve the problem completely. In 1830, partly inspired by the revolution in Paris, students and radical MPs in southern Germany began a protest movement calling for constitutional monarchy. In response, in 1832, Metternich passed the notorious six acts through the Frankfurt Diet which gave him the right to limit the powers of the parliaments of the various states in the Confederation. One way or another Metternich muzzled most opposition in Germany.

And yet even as the majority of anti-Austrian voices in Germany were being gagged, deeper historical processes, particularly in Prussia, were underway which would eventually threaten Habsburg hegemony. After the Congress of Vienna no one could have suspected that Prussia would eventually be the means by which Austria would be forced out of

Germany. The King of Prussia, Frederick William III, was a firm supporter of Austria and a willing partner in the Holy and Quadruple Alliances. Nevertheless, Prussia slowly began to undermine the Austrian position as a result of her growing economic strength. In 1834 she had set up a trading union which was joined by the majority of German states. This trading union, known as the Zollverein, was to become the basis of Prussian supremacy in Germany. Metternich wished to join the Zollverein but a combination of Prussian resistance to Austrian admission and Metternich's gradual realistion that Austrian industries might well suffer if exposed to competition in such a large free market meant that the Habsburgs remained permanently outside of the Zollverein.

Steadily Prussia began to industrialise and this in turn meant that she became a more potent military force. And yet during the Age of Metternich relations between Prussia and Austria remained largely harmonious. In that sense Metternich's German policy was a success. But it might well be offered as a criticism that Metternich was too busy silencing students and professors and was not sufficiently aware of the importance of industry. Ultimately, it might be argued, the ability to manufacture arms has a more profound impact than the ability to snoop on poets and daydreamers.

iii) The Revolutions of 1830 and the End of the Metternich System

In 1830 there was another revolution in France. Charles X was brought down and replaced by Louis Philippe as a constitutional monarch with considerably reduced powers. On hearing the news Metternich remarked, 'my whole life's work is destroyed'. He correctly feared that a French revolution would once again prove contagious. Within weeks there were revolts in Belgium, Switzerland, Poland, Germany and Italy.

Metternich was able to crush the uprisings in Germany and Italy with relative ease, treating them as essentially domestic issues. But above all he wanted to invoke the old Quadruple Alliance in order to suppress the French revolution and restore the absolute monarch Charles X. To this end he organised a conference of the great powers which met in London. But it proved a major disappointment. None of the other powers wanted to send troops into France, largely because they had revolutionary crises of their own with which to deal. In desperation Metternich planned an independent Austrian invasion of France, only to be informed by the high command that the army simply could not afford a war. The real weakness of Austria was suddenly apparent. The Metternich system it seems could only exist if other powers were prepared to do Metternich's fighting for him.

Metternich recognised his own impotence in 1830, remarking rather melodramatically that the French revolution marked the 'beginning of the end' for 'old Europe'. If a Metternich system can be said to have existed, it existed in foreign policy terms for 15 years after the Congress of Vienna. After 1830 Metternich never again appeared to provide the leadership of Europe. Even in the Mehemet Ali crisis of 1840 when concerted action by the great powers removed another threat to the Turkish Empire, it was Britain and not Austria that provided the strong leadership. During the crisis Metternich tried to resuscitate the old Congress System. But the British foreign minister, Lord Palmerston, preferred action to words and belittled Metternich for seeking to 'direct and instruct all the world' from his armchair. Evidently the Age of Metternich was drawing to a close.

6 Assessment: Was there a Metternich System?

It seems clear that Metternich was not in a position to dictate to either Europe or indeed Austria. The idea that he imposed his will upon all Europe is surely a gross exaggeration. There were very severe limitations on his effectiveness and influence both inside and outside of the Empire, all of which tended to leave him in a curiously weak position. Thus it might seem that the Metternich System is merely a creation of historians' imaginations.

However, such a simplistic answer will not suffice. As Sked has argued, in the last analysis this question depends on what is meant by the word 'system'. If 'system' implies that Metternich had absolute control over Habsburg society and the foreign policies of the Great Powers, then there was no system. But, as Sked argues, if 'system' means that Metternich had a broad strategy, underpinned loosely by classical conservatism, which was not always effective but which was pursued with a high degree of consistency, then yes, there was a system.

Making notes on 'The Age of Metternich'

The following questions should provide a useful framework for your notes. However, you must try to keep key issues and ideas in mind and not simply copy out informatiom. As you take notes ask yourself if you understand what you have just written. If you find that you are in doubt, go back to the book and re-read the relevant section.

Introduction: What were the ideas that Metternich opposed?
1   What sort of background did Metternich come from and how might this have influenced his political thinking
1.1 Describe the various social roles played by Metternich.
2   Why have historians changed the way that they have perceived and interpreted Metternich so much?
2.1 List the names of key historians and summarise briefly their views.
3   What was it that Metternich devoted his life to preserving?
3.1 Make brief notes for and against the view that Metternich's system was rooted in profound conservative philosophy.

4   What evidence is there to suggest that Metternich created a 'police state'?

4.1 Outline an argument against the view that Metternich created a 'police state'.

4.2 Define the two types of opposition movements in Hungary - you should be able to name the leader of each and list the main points of his reform programme.

4.3 How effectively did Metternich deal with these movements?

4.4 Why did Metternich find it so difficult to suppress Italian nationalism?

4.5 What grounds did Metternich have for saying that he did not govern Austria?

4.6 Why was Metternich so powerful between 1815 and 1835?

4.7 How and why did this situation change after 1835?

5   Explain why Metternich's initial approach (as foreign minister) to Napoleonic France was friendly.

5.1 What were Metternich's aims at the Congress of Vienna?

5.2 How successful was Metternich in defending the Vienna settlement before 1830?

5.3 What was Metternich's attitude to the German Confederation?

5.4 Why does the French revolution of 1830 perhaps mark the end of the Metternich system?

6   How does Alan Sked defend the idea of a Metternich system?

Answering essay questions on 'The Age of Metternich'

Many of the examination questions set on this period focus on the Congress of Vienna. (*The Concert of Europe* by John Lowe in this series will help you develop a broader understanding of the aims of the other states involved at Vienna.) The following questions are typical:

1   Were the statesmen at Vienna simply concerned to restore the pre-revolutionary order?

2   To what extent were the aims of the peacemakers at the Congress of Vienna achieved in the period 1815-48

3   How successful was Metternich in achieving his aims during the Congress of Vienna?

The way to approach questions of these sorts is to be sure what the aims of the various peacemakers at Vienna actually were. Make a list of the aims of each great power and another list of the ways in which they either did or did not fulfil their aims.

Notice that questions may simply be about the Congress or may involve an understanding of the longer-term consequences. Make a list of the possible long-term consequences of the Congress of Vienna.

If the questions are not about the Congress of Vienna, they will probably be about Metternich or the Empire more broadly. For example:

4   How successful was the Habsburg Empire in responding to the challenges facing it between 1815 and 1848?
5   Assess the effectiveness of Metternich's domestic policy between 1815 and 1848.

Clearly these questions are quite similar. But in what important respects do they differ? In both cases the 1848 revolutions are taken as the close of a period. It will not therefore be possible to do justice to these questions without looking at the next chapter on the 1848 revolutions.

Finally, there are sometimes questions on the Metternich system. Compose a short definition of the phrase and then make two lists: the arguments which support the view that such a system existed, and the counter arguments.

Source-based questions on 'The Age of Metternich'

1 The Character of Metternich
Carefully read the sources on page 16-18 and on pages 28-9. Answer the following questions.
a) Why do you think it is that Kolowrat cannot get on with Metternich? (3 marks)
b) Compare Metternich description of himself (page 16) with Kolowrat's assessment (page 29). How far do these sources provide reliable evidence to support the view that Metternich was an extremely vain and arrogant man? (7 marks)
c) Look at the portrait of Metternich on page 15. Describe the parts of the picture that suggest that Metternich was both a dandy and a figure of some importance. (5 marks)

2 Metternich's Ideology
Look at the extracts from Metternich writings on page 18. Answer the following questions.
a) How would Metternich's views on monarchy and the masses have affected his attitude towards constitutional reform? (6 marks)
b) Explain why Metternich did not like the principle of liberty. (4 marks)
c) Do you think that Metternich's principles constituted a workable political philosophy for the nineteenth century? Explain your answer. (5 marks)

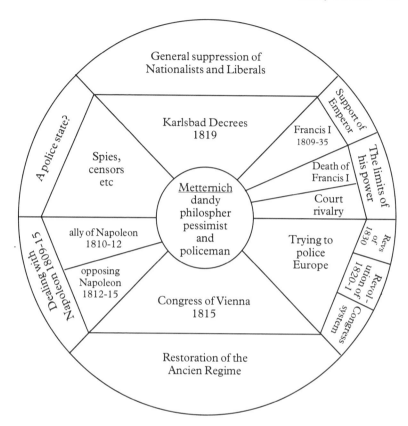

Summary - The Age of Metternich

CHAPTER 3

The Revolutions of 1848-9 in the Habsburg Empire

1 Introduction

In the spring of 1848 European history was at a turning point. Revolutions were sweeping across the continent with an apparently unstoppable momentum. They began in Paris. On 24 February Louis Philippe, the French King, was overthrown and a republic was established. Just over a fortnight later revolutions flared up in Bavaria, Prussia, Italy and throughout the Habsburg lands.

Indeed, the impact of the revolutionary movement in the Habsburg Empire had perhaps the most startling consequences of all the revolutions. At 9 pm on 13 March Prince Metternich resigned. Metternich had dedicated his political life to the prevention of revolution and the preservation of a centralised, absolutist political system dominated by the German speaking Austrian nobility. Hence his fall took on a kind of symbolic significance. It seemed to signal the end of the *Ancien Régime* and to promise the dawn of a new era.

Most historians agree that the forces which brought Metternich down were the relatively new creeds of nationalism and liberalism. The former was perhaps the most threatening to the Empire. After all, the Habsburg Monarchy was above all else a multi-national state. In 1848 the Hungarians, the Czechs and the Italians all pressed their claims for a greater measure of self-determination. As a result, revolutions broke out in Budapest, Prague, Milan and Venice. There was also a revolution in Vienna, but its emphasis was different in that it was motivated more by liberal pressures for constitutional reform. However, the distinction should not be exaggerated because most liberals also expected constitutional reform to increase the rights of the national groups within the Empire. In many cases a liberal was also a nationalist and *vice versa*. In short, the ideas which Metternich had been fighting to suppress ever since the fall of Napoleon now threatened to tear the Empire apart.

Yet, despite the fall of Metternich, the Habsburgs still managed to resist what seemed, for a brief moment, to be the irresistible forces of change. By the summer of 1849 all the revolutions had been suppressed. In fact, the common theme linking the revolutions across Europe turned out to be failure. But for some historians 1848 still represents a decisive moment. It was the 'turning point when Europe failed to turn'. Failure can be more significant than success. It has been argued that, by failing to reform itself in 1848, the Monarchy only bottled up problems which would destroy it totally in 1918.

2 The Revolutions of 1848-9: The Course of Events

It is an odd fact that the revolutions in the Habsburg Empire really began in France. The news that Louis Philippe and his chief minister, Guizot, had been overthrown on 24 February reached Vienna five days later. Such a momentous event immediately created enormous excitement: a mixture of hope that some sort of change would now take place in the Empire and fear that it might lead the authorities to clamp down even more severely.

Metternich was very worried by the turn of events. The removal of a king and the establishment of a republic was, in his eyes, a threat to the entire aristocratic social order which he had worked to preserve throughout his time in public life. He also knew only too well, from his memories of the Napoleonic era, the way in which revolutions begun in France had a habit of spreading to the rest of Europe. He toyed with the idea of military intervention in France to restore Louis Philippe but soon realised that the Monarchy had neither the funds nor the allies to embark on such a risky venture. Despite this concern, he remained confident, perhaps too confident, that he could contain any political problems that might arise within the Empire as a result of events in France.

However, the first sign that a storm was about to break came not in Austria but in Hungary. On 3 March, Louis Kossuth, leader of the Hungarian nationalist movement, made a powerful speech in the lower house of the Hungarian Diet at Pozsony. He called for self-government for Hungary through the establishment of a new parliament in Budapest. He did not, at this stage, call for separation or independence but his draft of reform proposals would have left the Emperor as little more than a figurehead. He then went on to claim that this was the 'right' of all the historic nations within the Empire. In effect he called for the complete dismantling of the old system. For many this was just the rallying cry they wanted to hear. Copies of Kossuth's speech were soon circulating in Vienna. It was the kind of manifesto to which liberals and nationalists alike could subscribe.

a) The Fall of Metternich

Kossuth's speech led to speculation that when the lower house of the Austrian Diet next met on 13 March there would be similar calls for radical reform. The coincidence that this also happened to be carnival week in Vienna may have contributed to the atmosphere of giddy optimism.

On Sunday 12 March the university students of Vienna gathered to draft a petition calling for numerous liberal reforms. They were supported by their professors, in particular Hye and Endlicher. These two 'intellectuals' presented the petition to the Emperor's adviser and uncle, Archduke Ludwig. No promise was made but the students felt that they had had a sympathetic hearing and this encouraged them to think that the court might be in the mood to accept change.

Metternich remained remarkably calm. In fact this was dangerous complacency, especially when it is remembered that the Viennese garrison, perhaps the last line of defence in a revolutionary situation, was under the command of the incompetent Archduke Albrecht. On the other hand, the people, whether they were students, workers or respectable burghers, felt instinctively that the next day, Monday 13 March, would be decisive one way or another.

On Monday the lower house of the Austrian Diet duly met in the Landhaus on the Herrengasse in central Vienna, less than half a mile from the Hofburg, the Imperial palace. A huge crowd, consisting of all manner of social groups ranging from the criminal to the intellectual, gathered outside the building. Whilst the members of the Diet tried to debate the whole issue of reform, the crowd outside grew increasingly restless. Another figure who has been called an 'intellectual' (although he was a medical doctor rather than an academic one) made a name for himself as an orator calling for liberal reforms and parliaments for all the nationalities. He was Dr Adolf Fischof. He roused the assembled crowd to fever pitch by quoting extracts from Kossuth's great speech of 3 March. Attempts by the students to burst into the building and the general noise and disturbance eventually led to the meeting breaking up. The members of the Diet decided to pass the buck. They informed the Emperor of the crowd's feelings and demands, in particular of the intensity of the popular hatred for Metternich, and then bowed out. The huge mob, sensing a tactical victory, moved on to the Imperial palace itself.

Inside the palace, Ferdinand could hear the chants of the crowd. From this he could tell that above all they wanted the dismissal of Metternich, but also that they were still prepared to cheer at the mention of the Emperor's name. Ferdinand was widely regarded as weak and mentally deficient, a judgement inspired only partly by his epileptic fits, but precisely because of this he was not blamed for Imperial policies. Imbecility was at this stage the Emperor's strongest card. Metternich was seen as the real ruler and as such he was the target of the crowd's hostility. The crowd at this point was not violent but it was certainly a threat to law and order. Some of the more unscrupulous demonstrators also indulged in looting. Archduke Albrecht moved troops into the area to try to ensure the security of the palace itself. According to one contemporary observer Albrecht was then hit on the head by an iron lantern bracket and forced to retire, thus leaving the troops temporarily without leadership. This may well explain why a contingent of Italian soldiers panicked and opened fire on the mob, killing four people. The generally peaceful protest turned instantly into a riot. Metternich's house was attacked and the Emperor, faced with this crisis, was left with two clear alternatives: to give in to the people's demands or use force to suppress the rioters. At this pivotal moment the role of Ferdinand's advisers became crucial.

Metternich was usually able to rely on the support of the effective regent, Archduke Ludwig. But within the court there was a very distinct anti-Metternich faction. This was led by Archduke John, Ludwig's brother, who had established a reputation as a liberal. In conjunction with Kolowrat, Metternich's main rival on the Council of State, he sought to exploit the moment and persuade the Emperor and, perhaps more importantly, Archduke Ludwig that the time was right for dropping the aged chancellor.

However, although there was a court conspiracy against Metternich the decisive factor in changing Ludwig's attitude seems to have been the petition brought to him by the almost exclusively middle-class Civic Guard. These eminently respectable men told Ludwig that, if the troops were withdrawn and Metternich dismissed, they, in conjunction with the students, would promise to restore order and political stability. Ludwig then advised the bewildered Ferdinand that it would be wise to let Metternich go. And so at 9 pm on Monday 13 March, Prince Metternich, after delivering a speech which lasted for over an hour to the Emperor and his court, finally came to the point and resigned. Other concessions quickly followed. The Civic Guard was renamed the National Guard, so that its members would feel more important, and the students were given arms and the grand new title of the 'Academic Legion' - in reality a shambolic bunch of young romantics led by a retired military man of whom very little notice was taken.

The fall of Metternich ushered in the triumphant phase of the revolution. The Monarchy was thrown onto the defensive. Ferdinand may have granted some concessions but these had by no means entirely satisfied the appetites of the reformers for change. In fact, rather the reverse was true. Metternich's departure encouraged liberals and nationalists throughout the Empire to press their case even more aggressively, sensing the weakness of the Emperor's position. On 15 March, in an attempt to placate the people, the Emperor put out a statement promising a new constitution and appointed a new ministry with the specific task of producing it. Kolowrat somewhat reluctantly accepted the position of Minister-President but the responsibility for the new constitution was Count Pillersdorf's at the Ministry of the Interior.

b) The April Laws

Before a new constitution could be patched together the revolution spread to other parts of the Empire. After the fall of Metternich the Hungarians immediately began demanding concessions, such as a parliament with far greater powers and a long list of liberal reforms including freedom of the press, trial by jury and non-interference in the education system. Kossuth wished to go further and pressed for the abolition of serfdom, sensing quite correctly that this would put the Hungarian peasantry on the side of the revolution. He also wished to alter the constitutional relationship between Hungary and the crown. Hungary would have its own bi-cameral parliament with a lower chamber elected by all males over 20 and an aristocratic upper chamber. This parliament would in effect be sovereign, although Hungary would still swear loyalty to the Emperor. However, the Monarch would be unable to introduce any legislation affecting Hungary without the approval of its parliament. In short, Ferdinand would become a royal figurehead with no real authority in Hungary. At first Ferdinand and his advisers resisted Kossuth's proposals, but eventually the court decided that obstruction would only lead in the end to the complete fragmentation of the Empire, and therefore conceded to Kossuth's reform demands. Ferdinand officially ratified this constitutional package on 11 April, and hence these are known as the 'April Laws'. The April Laws were nothing short of a constitutional revolution. The Magyars had achieved almost complete control over their affairs, including the vital matter of finance. Their willingness to continue to swear loyalty to the crown was only a polite gesture, a fig leaf to save the Habsburgs from political embarrassment.

However, even in this triumphal phase of the revolution, the Magyars had sowed the seeds of their future defeat. The 'April Laws' brought new national 'rights' for Hungarians only. But there were numerous southern Slav groups living within what the Magyars called the Kingdom of St. Stephen - the area to which Kossuth laid claim. These felt cheated because, for example, fluency in the Magyar language was necessary in order to be allowed to vote. The Croats, in particular, resented Magyar domination. The Croatian governor, General Jellačić, privately refused to recognise the legality of the April Laws but, because Ferdinand had put his name to the new constitution, he felt obliged at least to appear to accept it. He had no wish to come into conflict with the Monarchy. However, he judged correctly that the mood of the court would change. Eventually it came to see Croatian nationalism as a means to put down the nationalism of the Magyars.

c) The Second Viennese Revolution

The fall of Metternich is often referred to as the first revolution in Vienna. But on 15 May there was another popular rising which can be seen as a second revolution. The cause of this new outbreak of demonstrations was widespread dissatisfaction with the promised constitution which had been published on 25 April. It was largely the work of Count Pillersdorf, the Minister of the Interior. The new constitution is usually regarded as inept. Pillersdorf misjudged the mood of the people and produced a constitutional blueprint which was too conservative to meet with popular approval. The Czechs and the Italians wanted what the Hungarians seemed to have: sovereign national parliaments of their own. Instead, Pillersdorf offered a central Imperial parliament to which each national group could send representatives. But the parliament was to be elected on a narrow franchise and the Emperor was to retain the right to veto any legislation of which he disapproved. All groups found something in it to reject. However, the main objection was shared by all the reformers. They did not want to see the old tradition of centralised rule from Vienna continue. This smacked of the old bureaucratic and autocratic system. The Pillersdorf constitution, so impatiently awaited, seemed to be a betrayal. Disillusionment swiftly turned to anger.

The anger led to a public demonstration on 15 May against the proposed constitution. For a second time a crowd gathered outside the Hofburg palace. They demanded a different constitution. Ferdinand once more gave way. A new document was promised and riotous celebrations followed. To many in the court it seemed that they were almost prisoners in their own home. The armed students in the Academic Legion and the bourgeois National Guard had control of the streets. Indeed, power itself now seemed to be in the hands of the people rather than the Emperor. Archduchess Sophie, the wife of Ferdinand's brother Francis Charles, wrote in her diary, 'we are like a mouse in a trap here'. The ladies at court took the initiative. Ferdinand was advised that Vienna was no longer a safe place for him to remain. On 17 May the Emperor and his court fled from Vienna to the safety of Innsbruck. Governmental authority in domestic matters was passed to the newly established Committee of Public Safety, presided over by Dr Fischof. For the next three months the Committee ruled Vienna.

The Emperor's flight, though perhaps not necessary, seemed to clarify the political issues somewhat. Whereas before it was possible to claim loyalty to the Monarchy and still demand change, now it seemed that one was either for or against the Empire. The time for compromise had suddenly passed. Many among the cautious middle classes began to panic. Divisions opened up between radical and conservative reformers. The revolution began to show signs of weakness and uncertainty. Ironically, the Emperor had made a shrewd political move without realising it. However, his fate was now in the hands of the only group which might realistically reverse the revolution - the army.

d) Events in Italy

The transformation of the reform movement into a military struggle between revolutionaries and the army had already taken place in Northern Italy. In fact, Lombardy and Venetia had been under martial law for some time as a result of the fighting which had broken out in January 1848 between civilians and soldiers during the boycott of tobacco, a state monopoly, organised by the nationalists. In addition, there was a renewed spirit of Italian nationalism present, partly as a result of the apparent support of the new pope, Pius IX, for liberal and nationalist causes. The news of Metternich's resignation sparked nationalist uprisings in Milan and Venice in March. The 82-year-old commander of the Austrian forces, Marshal Radetzky, was forced to withdraw from Milan on 22 March. In Venice Daniel Manin led a similar patriotic revolt. The rebellious towns looked to Charles Albert, King of Piedmont-Sardinia, for support in their effort to break away from the Empire. Piedmont-Sardinia was an independent north Italian state which bordered on the Empire. Charles Albert, who had acquired a reputation as a liberal after introducing a new constitution in his kingdom in February 1848, hoped to exploit the weakness of the Austrian army and capture Lombardy and Venetia. But he was motivated less by liberalism than by the ambition to transform Piedmont-Sardinia into a major European power. He marched into Lombardy on 23 March with an army of 60,000 men. This was considerably larger than Radetzky's army and many observers felt at this time that the Monarchy's best policy would be to cut its losses and admit defeat. Radetzky was appalled to learn that Vienna seriously considered this policy and that the government ministers were thinking in terms of giving up Lombardy in order to concentrate the military effort on the retaking of Venetia. Radetzky was relieved to discover that neither the Lombards nor Charles Albert were prepared to accept such a compromise. Radetzky had one thing in his favour. He still controlled the four fortresses of Peschiera, Mantua, Verona and Legnano. This was the famous Quadrilateral, the key to the security of Lombardy and Venetia. In the late spring of 1848 Radetzky was able to regroup here and await a change of mood at court which might lead to the sending of reinforcements.

e) Prague: The Turning Point

The first major defeat for the revolution came not in Vienna, Budapest or the Italian cities, but in Prague. In March the Czechs, inspired by the Hungarians and led by Palacký, pressed their claim for a national parliament. The Imperial government made some concessions, including abolishing the laws which made it illegal for Czech speakers to occupy positions of influence such as army officers or in the upper echelons of the civil service. Vague promises were also made about a parliamentary body. In June Palacký opened the so-called first Slav Congress. This institution was not in any way intended to be a challenge to the authority of Vienna. Indeed, one of the characteristics of Czech nationalism as led by Palacký was its continual assertion of loyalty to the Empire. In some ways the Slav Congress was a defensive response to the Frankfurt parliament, in which German representatives discussed the various possible ways of unifying Germany and which seemed to want to subsume the Czech people into a new German state. Palacký was profoundly opposed to this, just as he was bitterly hostile to Russian ambitions to lead some sort of Panslav union. The odd result of this was that Palacký came to feel that the Empire was the best guarantee of security the Czechs had. Palacký wanted a federal constitution which would give the Czechs a greater measure of self-determination whilst remaining under the protective cloak of the Empire. This policy has been called 'Austroslavism'.

The Slav Congress met on 2 June. It was unable to achieve very much simply because it existed for such a short time. On 12 June riots broke out in Prague. They had almost nothing to do with the Congress, being essentially a protest by unemployed workers about the introduction of new machinery. The working-class rioters were joined by radical students, but there is no reason to suppose that Palacký and his supporters were connected with the rioters. General Windischgraetz, commander of the Imperial army in Prague and fierce opponent of the revolution, seized this opportunity to put down what he regarded as yet another manifestation of the revolution. The city was bombarded and then occupied by his troops. Following this, the members of the Slav Congress as well as the rioters were ruthlessly silenced. Windischgraetz's severity can partly be explained by the fact that his wife was killed by a stray bullet during the early stages of the fighting. The Czech national movement was snuffed out and the severity of the consequent trials for treason was clearly meant to be a lesson for the rest of the Empire's unruly subjects. The forcible closure of the Slav Congress proved to be a decisive turning point in the history of the 1848 revolutions in the Habsburg Empire.

f) The Defeat of the Italians

The news of Windischgraetz's triumph gave heart to the Emperor and his court at Innsbruck. It led them to look at the pleas for reinforcements to be sent to northern Italy in a new light. Radetzky was gradually able to swell his army to over 50,000. But Windischgraetz refused to send any troops from Prague and in the summer of 1848 it still seemed unlikely that it would be possible to defeat the Italians. But the 82 year-old-Field Marshal was determined to try. The result was a brilliant victory for the Imperial army over Charles Albert's force at Custoza on 25 July. Radetzky marched back into Milan and took the city with little resistance. He then laid siege to Venice. The Venetians, led by Daniel Manin, held out for a year but eventually a combination of cholera and cannon fire forced them to surrender in August 1849.

Windischgraetz and, especially, Radetzky had between them reversed the fortunes of the Emperor. The Italians had, after all, posed a genuine threat to the unity of the Empire whereas the Czechs were essentially loyal. This has led some historians to argue that Radetzky was the real saviour of the Empire and that Custozza was the most significant turning point.

g) The October Days in Vienna

The summer in Vienna was a particularly tense time. An Imperial parliament met on 22 July. This was a modified version of Pillersdorf's original concept of a central assembly - the main difference being that this was a single chamber parliament elected on the basis of universal suffrage. However, the parliament spent most of its time debating the *minutiae* of constitutional procedure and therefore passed little legislation of significance. Its main achievement was the abolition of serfdom in the Empire, but even this was in some ways a mixed blessing since in many cases the newly-freed rural workers joined the movement of labourers into the towns, thereby increasing the number of urban unemployed. The Committee of Public Safety under Dr Fischof sought ways to reduce the suffering of the jobless. Emulating France, they set

This French cartoon helps to explain why the Empire survived the 1848 revolution. From left to right the generals are Jellačič, Radetzky and Windischgraetz

up National Workshops which were supposed to provide useful work with pay.

On 12 August Ferdinand returned to Vienna feeling that the worst excesses of the revolution were now over. He had miscalculated again. By the end of the month the streets were filled with demonstrators protesting about the Committee's failure to solve the problem of unemployment and the inadequacy of the National Workshops. The workshops had proved too costly and Dr Fischof had reluctantly agreed to cut pay rates. This action had brought the workers and students onto the streets, making the divisions in the revolutionary movement very apparent. Fischof was experiencing some of the problems of power. Many of his bourgeois supporters felt that demonstrators were going too far. On the other hand, the more radical students and the workers felt that the revolution was being betrayed by the timidity of its new leaders.

In September General Jellačič's Croatian army finally attacked the Hungarians. Seeing the success of Windischgraetz and Radetzky, Jellačič judged the time right to assault the Magyars. But it was the response of the Court and the government in Vienna to this action, rather than the action itself, which led to the violence of the October Days. Ferdinand and the minister in charge of foreign affairs, Wessenberg, made no attempt to restrain Jellačič, who was after all fighting to abolish a constitution signed and approved by the Emperor. Many in Vienna suspected that the authorities were hoping that Jellačič would crush the Hungarian revolution. Their fears were confirmed when on 3 October the Emperor took the dramatic step of pronouncing the Hungarian Diet officially dissolved. The Court also stated that the April Laws had been illegal.

Kossuth, the hero of the early stage of the revolution, now declared the revolution in danger. He appointed himself Chairman of the Hungarian Committee for National Defence and called all opponents of reaction to act now to save the cause. This led to what might be called the third revolution in Vienna. On 6 October the people massed on the streets in such numbers that violence was almost inevitable. Matters came to a head when the mob sought to prevent a regiment of soldiers being sent by train from Vienna to Hungary to aid Jellačič. Fighting broke out and there were a few casualties. The soldiers retreated and the angry crowd marched on the Ministry of War. They forced entry and the helpless minister, Count Latour, who was rumoured to be orchestrating the counter-revolution, was hunted down in his own building and brutally murdered. His naked body was strung up from a lamp post. Not surprisingly, the court once again fled the capital - this time to Olmütz in Moravia.

The Empire and the dynasty was once again to be preserved by the military men. On 24 October Windischgraetz began to attack the city of Vienna. After a week's fighting and with the assistance of Jellačič's forces, Windischgraetz finally 'liberated' the city. Over two thousand people were killed during the October Days. Afterwards the leaders of the resistance were rounded up and, after a brief court martial, shot. The Academic Legion and the Committee of Public Safety were dissolved. The revolution in Vienna was over. Only the Hungarians remained defiant. Before turning his attention to Budapest, Windischgraetz decided to attack what he saw as the root of all the problems: weakness at the top. His brother-in-law, Prince Felix Schwarzenberg, was placed in control of the government. The General was also insistent that the Empire could no longer be left in the hands of a half-wit. Ferdinand was persuaded of the need for his abdication. This he did in December in favour of his 18-year-old nephew, Franz Joseph, who was to wear the crown until his death in 1916 when the Empire was all but finished.

Thus, at the end of this most tumultuous of years, the Empire emerged with a strengthened political leadership and all her territory intact, although the Hungarians and the Venetians still proclaimed themselves independent. The political situation was, not surprisingly, rather confused, particularly when in December 1848 Schwarzenberg proclaimed that he was still in favour of some form of 'constitutional monarchy'. Indeed, he encouraged the Imperial parliament, now meeting at Kremsier, to continue its attempt to draft a new workable constitution. Whether this was a cynical deception by Schwarzenberg or whether he changed his views under pressure from Windischgraetz and the Emperor is hard to say, but when the Kremsier constitution was presented in January 1849 it led only to the immediate dissolution of the parliament and the arrest of some of its more radical members, including Dr Fischof. The revolutionary wheel had come full circle: absolute monarchy in the person of Franz Joseph had emerged as an apparently reborn and renewed institution.

The loose ends were finally tied up when the Venetians and the Hungarians were both defeated. The Hungarians were finally crushed at the battle of Világos in August 1849 and Venice capitulated later the same month. A major factor in the victory over the Hungarians was the assistance given to the Habsburgs by the Russian army. Tsar Nicholas I had responded to the Emperor's call for help partly out of monarchical solidarity and partly because he thought Hungarian success might lead the Poles under Russian rule to seek a similar independence. However, important as Russian intervention was, the decisive underlying factor in Hungary's defeat was its lack of industrial capacity to produce enough arms with which to fight a lengthy war. The rebels were treated very badly by the invading Austrian army, but Kossuth managed to escape into permanent exile. The departure of the man whose speech had sparked the revolution in March 1848 signalled the end of the revolutionary period.

3 The Causes of the Revolutions

a) Population Growth and the Agricultural Crisis

In the first half of the nineteenth century the population of the Habsburg Empire rose dramatically. This in itself partly explains why so many social problems, such as food shortages, unemployment and overcrowding in the cities, seemed to occur at this time. Vienna, the political heart of the Empire and the site of one of the major revolutions, doubled its population between 1815 and 1848. However, this demographic explosion produced a crisis firstly in the rural areas. Three-quarters of the inhabitants of the Empire lived and worked in the countryside where rapid population growth produced an agricultural crisis in the 1840s when production levels failed to keep pace with the increase in the number of people. Although this did not affect all parts of the Empire, and there are sources which suggest that some of the peasantry in the more fertile regions survived comfortably, some sectors of the rural community, such as the seasonally-employed landless labourers, faced starvation.

This already difficult situation grew suddenly worse in the three years before the revolutions. In 1845 there was a bad harvest, but in 1846 and 1847 the harvest failed almost completely. This was partly because of floods, but 1846 was also the year of the notorious potato blight in Europe. In some regions of the Empire the potato was the main item of diet for the peasantry. In addition, in Hungary an outbreak of cattle plague ruined the livelihoods of many. Shortage of basic foods led to an increase in prices, while high rates of taxation on consumables exacerbated the problem and helped to make the government very unpopular. Unable to survive where they were living, many of the hungry made their way into the towns hoping to find work in the new factories. This partly explains the dramatic rise in the population of Vienna, and the other major cities, which was in many ways the consequence of an agricultural crisis.

b) The Slow Rate of Industrialisation

Unfortunately the Empire did not have sufficient industrial capacity to offset the impact of the agricultural crisis. Compared to most of western Europe the Empire was relatively backward economically and, despite the fact that annual growth rates in the cotton and mining industries were as high as 7 per cent in parts of Lower Austria and Bohemia, there was simply not enough work in the towns to absorb the rapid influx of labour. As a result unemployment rose sharply. The government itself was also economically very weak. State finances were in deficit and only loans from private bankers such as the Rothschilds prevented the government from going bankrupt. The chronic debts of the government encouraged many to call for major reforms of a monarchical system that seemed wasteful and inefficient.

c) The Social Discontents of the Urban Poor

There can be no doubt that it was the poorer working-class elements in the towns which made up the 'mob' element in the revolution. Their discontent stemmed from the harshness of the conditions in which they had to live. The outlying districts of Vienna, for example, were notorious centres of crime, poverty, drunkenness, disease and all the other social evils associated with early industrialisation. These conditions for the working class were exacerbated by the constant threat of unemployment. On the eve of the revolution there were at least 10,000 unemployed people in Vienna and food prices were soaring. As a result, the mood of the working class was extremely volatile. Indeed, the very presence of the 'unwashed' working classes, with their attendant hooligan element, in the wealthier parts of Vienna was enough to start a panic and it could be argued that Metternich's fall was brought about, very largely, because of the ability of the crowd to intimidate the authorities. Clearly then, conditions in the major cities fomented revolution. It is no accident that every city with a population of over 100,000 experienced some sort of revolutionary activity. However although the threat from the working classes was an important factor it should be emphasised that this class did not provide the leaders of the revolution. The urban poor did not have a clear set of aims. They only had a sense of injustice which attracted them to any movement which promised change.

d) The Rebellion of the Middle and Upper Classes

The leaders of the revolution were drawn from the middle and upper classes. However, the role of these classes differed considerably in each of the four distinct sites of revolutionary activity. Nevertheless, a pattern can be discerned. In those areas which most resented rule from Vienna, namely the Italian and Hungarian territories, the landed classes seem to have been the leading revolutionary element. But in those areas whose aims were more reformist than revolutionary, namely the Czech lands and Austria itself, the leaders of events were primarily from the middle class. There are of course exceptions to this pattern but it is broadly accurate.

In Vienna and Prague, for example, the leaders of the reform movement, such as Dr Fischof and Palacký, were solidly middle-class, and they were by no means isolated examples. Indeed, it was largely the educated middle classes, such as lawyers, journalists, and university professors, who were most active in criticising the existing system. In many cases middle-class rebels were prompted by very lofty ideals. Palacký, for example, sincerely believed in the rights and the destiny of the Czech people, while Dr Fischof sincerely believed in constitutional reform. Hence some historians, such as Sir Lewis Namier in *The Revolution of the Intellectuals*, have tended to criticise the middle-class leaders and their student followers because they were theorists and dreamers rather than practical men of action. Whilst there is some truth in this accusation, and it helps to explain the eventual failure of the revolution, it would be wrong to overlook more basic middle-class motivations.

Even without liberal or nationalist beliefs, the professional middle class had sufficient material reasons to want to change the system. They were in very many cases employed by the government and their salaries, compared to the self-employed middle class, were very low - this explains why the professional sector of the middle class was far more active in the revolution than the industrial and commercial elements. They blamed the government's financial incompetence for their poor pay. Metternich in particular had a reputation for wasting money on needless military projects. In addition, it was felt that the government as an employer discriminated in favour of German-speaking members of the nobility and therefore that the highest posts were effectively barred to members of the middle class. Thus it seemed to many that getting rid of Metternich and reforming the administration as a whole would lead in the end to an improvement in their financial position.

The role of the middle classes has been allowed by many historians to overshadow the role of the aristocracy. However, as Alan Sked has argued, if any one class deserves the label 'revolutionary' then that class is the nobility in Hungary and Italy. For example, Louis Kossuth, the best-known revolutionary to emerge in 1848, was a member of the lesser nobility. The Italian aristocracy in Lombardy and Venetia particularly resented being treated as subordinate to the Austrian aristocracy. Many Italian titles for example were either simply not recognised by Austrians or were downgraded. Italian dukes were treated as mere counts when in Vienna. But in neighbouring Piedmont Charles Albert made a particular point of recognising the Lombard nobility and offering them and their sons the kind of career opportunities in the army or the bureaucracy denied to them by the Habsburgs. This explains why the Lombard nobility not only invited Charles Albert to join them in fighting against the Austrian forces in 1848 but also why there was such a willingness amongst the nobility to exchange rule by the Habsburgs for rule by the house of Savoy.

Ironically, Metternich was well aware of the resentment felt by the Italian aristocracy and monitored the situation very carefully. However, he could not believe that they would be foolish enough to dabble with revolution. He assumed that everyone else remembered the lessons of the French Revolution as keenly as he did. A letter he wrote in January 1848 made this quite clear:

1 What do the Lombard nobility want? Do they intend to renounce their moral and material existence? How can they do so? Yet their conduct must make one assume this. The driving force behind the unspeakable position of the country is coming without a shadow of
5 a doubt from their side. Do they want to surrender their fortunes on the high altar of some incredible divinity and bring on the holocaust? Do they intend to support that party which today can only triumph at the cost of their life and prosperity? They cannot want that. Otherwise they do not know how to judge what they
10 want or where they are going.

Clearly Metternich could not quite bring himself to believe that the Lombard aristocracy would really want to rebel against the Empire. His touching faith in the loyalty of his own class was perhaps his biggest miscalculation. The views expressed by Felix Schwarzenberg, the man who eventually inherited Metternich's position in the Empire, writing to Windischgraetz after the revolution, clearly showed that the government had now learnt that they could no longer rely on the class loyalty of the non-Austrian nobility in the way that Metternich had:

1 I do not believe in political conversions and since the nobility in Hungary made and executed the revolution there, I find no guarantee of its future effectiveness. One can be of old lineage, have an old title and call oneself an aristocrat but still be a
5 supporter of revolutionary subversion.

Interestingly, although Schwarzenberg did not see the Austrian aristocracy as revolutionary or subversive, he did see them, exactly as most members of the middle class did, as politically incompetent.

1 I know of not a dozen men of our class with sufficient political wisdom or with the necessary experience to whom an important share of power could be entrusted without soon having to fear for it. I have thought a great deal about how to constitute the
5 aristocracy of Austria as a body so as to maintain for it an appropriate political influence, but the elements out of which this body consists, I have been unable to find. Democracy must be fought and its excesses must be challenged but in the absence of other means of help, that can only be done by the government
10 itself. To rely on an ally as weak as our aristocracy unfortunately is, would be to damage our cause more than help it.

Clearly then, contemporaries recognised the primary role played by the aristocracy in the revolutions. However, in order to understand the role of both the nobility and the middle class fully it is important to examine the ideologies which motivated them.

e) The Influence of Nationalism and Liberalism

An empire that was made up of at least eleven different national groups was clearly threatened by the rise of nationalism. Despite Metternich's attempts to censor and restrict the spread of such ideas, nationalist opinions and attitudes gradually permeated the literate classes. The nationalist movement was very strong in Hungary, Italy and the Czech lands. However, these three movements were very different, particularly in terms of their political aims. At one extreme, many Italians wanted complete separation from the Empire whilst at the other extreme, the Czechs wanted to remain firmly within the Empire but with some form of home rule. Hungarian nationalism changed rapidly as the revolution developed, becoming steadily more radical until, like the Italians, the Hungarians eventually sought to break away altogether, having begun as essentially loyal. It is therefore very important to distinguish between these various strains of nationalism.

The intellectual leader of the Czech national movement was Frantisek Palacký. As a historian he sought to remind Czechs of their historic and cultural identity. His letter to the Frankfurt parliament in April 1848 revealed much about the nature of his nationalism:

1 I am a Czech of Slavonic blood, and with all the little I possess and
   all the little I can do, I have devoted myself for all time to the
   service of my nation. That nation is a small one, it is true, but from
   time immemorial it has been a nation of itself and based upon its
5 own strength ... it is your irrevocable desire and purpose to
   undermine Austria as an independent empire and indeed to make
   her impossible for all time to come - an empire whose preservation,
   integrity and consolidation is, and must be, a great and important
   matter for my own nation but also for humanity and civilisation
10 itself.

Clearly Palacký was essentially loyal to the Empire. He wanted a greater measure of self-government within a more federal constitution rather than independence.

Italian and Hungarian nationalism tended to be of a more aggressive nature. The main inspiration behind the Italian nationalist movement was Giuseppe Mazzini. Although he was only briefly involved with the rising in Milan and left there in order to lead the revolution in Rome, his propaganda set the tone for nationalism in northern Italy. Several years before the revolution Mazzini had set out the demands of Italian nationalists:

1 We demand to exist. We demand a name. We desire to make our
country powerful and respected, free and happy ... in other words,
we demand independence, unity, and liberty for ourselves and for
our fellow countrymen. All are agreed in the cry of 'Out with the
5 foreigner'.

However, Italian nationalism took a number of different forms, from
Mazzini's romantic dream of a revolution which would somehow usher
in a democratic, fully-unified Italian republic to the more pragmatic
designs of D'Azeglio, Piedmont's prime minister, to create a federation
of Italian states which would be dominated by Piedmont. The King of
Piedmont, Charles Albert, also supported D'Azeglio's approach and
looked at Lombardy and Venetia as possible extensions to his territories
which might be legitimately 'liberated' from Habsburg control in the
name of Italian nationalism. Nevertheless, most Italian nationalists in
Lombardy and Venetia welcomed the assistance of Piedmont. In stark
contrast to the Czechs, the Italian nationalists wanted independence
and because of this the revolutions in Milan and Venice must be seen as
a serious challenge to the territorial integrity of the Empire. In Hungary
the Magyars wanted to exercise complete political control over what
they termed the ancient Kingdom of St. Stephen. This amounted to
radical constitutional change if not quite separation.

Most nationalists were also liberals precisely because liberals
favoured constitutional reform and many nationalists thought that this
would be the means by which their nation might achieve a greater
measure of independence. Liberals believed in creating a new
constitution with an elected parliament and a monarch who would be
subject to that parliament. In other words, they wanted constitutional
rather than absolute monarchy. They also believed in certain basic rights
and freedoms such as the right to free speech, a free press, free trade and
the need for laws to be made which enshrined these principles. Their
belief in equality before the law made them enemies of the privileges
enjoyed by socialites: not surprisingly it tended to be members of the
middle class who supported liberal ideas because they resented the
privileges enjoyed by the landed classes. Although this was in theory a
revolutionary programme, in that it required a constitutional revolution,
in practice most liberals did not believe in violence and they most
certainly did not want to cause a bloody revolution. Most liberals were
propertied middle-class men who feared that a revolution might allow
the masses to acquire power. Thus there is a paradox about liberalism in
1848: in some ways it was a great threat to the existing autocratic system,
but in other ways it was a support, acting as a buffer against violent or
far-reaching change. Their modest desires for reform turned into
revolution because they became entangled with nationalist passions and
also with the small but dynamic 'radical' movement.

The radicals wanted to see the introduction of universal suffrage and the recognition of the 'right to work', hence the introduction of National Workshops during the radical phase of the revolution. The students were the most radical group and also the loudest. They enjoyed organising noisy demonstrations and wrote scandalous pamphlets mocking the government. The radicals were always in a minority with more ideas than discipline, but they were able to attract support from some of the working class enabling them often to put the force of the mob behind their arguments. However this political alliance was always a fragile one, educated students and poor labourers having little in common, and in the end the Academic Legion proved to be better at insulting their opponents than fighting them.

These then were the essential factors which helped create the revolutions. The social tensions brought about by industrialisation and population growth are perhaps best regarded as underlying causes which created the conditions in which liberal and nationalist ideas could thrive. However, it is also true that entirely unpredictable elements conspired to create a revolutionary situation. For example, the fall of Louis Philippe, the rash behaviour of the troops in Vienna and the peculiar idiocy of the Emperor were all in a sense accidents which befell the Empire. Metternich's fall, for example, was not necessarily inevitable despite all the problems which converged on Vienna in March 1848: arguably the behind-the-scenes court rivalries are just as important as any of the profound underlying problems in explaining his fall.

Clearly then one must be wary of simple answers: there is no easy explanation for the events of 1848. Each of the revolutions in the Empire was, in some respects, a unique event and what applies to one may not apply to another. Essentially 1848 in the Habsburg Empire saw a number of quite different attempts to force major constitutional change on the Monarchy. Though very different, they came to share one common feature - failure.

4 The Failure of the Revolutions

Why did so much activity achieve so little? The main reason why the revolutions failed was because the army, led by Windischgraetz and Radetzky, was able to crush the rebels. The Habsburg Monarchy owed its continued existence very largely to the stubborn determination of these two men and in particular to Radetzky whose defeat of the Italians was the real psychological turning point in the Monarchy's fortunes. However, Ferdinand's decision to give in to the reformers, although it may have seemed spineless to Windischgraetz, does in retrospect appear to have been a wise tactical retreat, albeit one prompted more by panic than cunning. In addition to this, the fact that the revolutionaries were not united in their aims weakened their efforts considerably. Tensions between the differing sorts of nationalism precluded the emergence of any form of co-operation between non-German opponents of the regime. Czech and Italian nationalists, for example, had very little in common and indeed the Monarchy eventually found that it could use nationalism to defend itself against nationalism - using Jellačič's Croatian nationalists against the Magyars. Divisions amongst liberals and radicals, particularly about the National Workshops, soon led reformers like Dr Fischof into conflict with the more extreme students. These internal struggles in the reform movement were further exacerbated by underlying class tensions. The middle-class reformers had a very ambivalent attitude to the working class as political allies: they were seen as a useful means of intimidating the authorities but they were also regarded as politically dangerous in that they naturally inclined to the radical cause which went far beyond the aims of the middle classes. In addition, the flirtation with mob violence unnerved many of the more educated middle-class reformers and events like the brutal lynching of Latour caused many of the more faint-hearted either to give up the cause entirely or even actively to oppose the revolution. Therefore opponents of the system were not unified whilst for the Generals the restoration of order gave a clear purpose. External factors, such as changing circumstances in Paris, also helped to alter the situation inside the Empire. News of the defeat of the French radicals during the June Days gave Windischgraetz the signal he wanted and ultimately, of course, the strength of the army proved to be the decisive factor.

5 Consequences

Perhaps the main lasting achievement of the revolution was the legal abolition of serfdom in the Empire, but oddly this measure succeeded precisely because it was never a major issue and would probably have occurred without a revolution given the widespread support for it within the nobility. In most other respects the consequences of the revolutions were rather negative. In many ways 1848 was a missed opportunity to reform the centralised and absolutist political structure of the Empire. It is possible to argue that in 1848 the forces of liberalism received a blow from which they never recovered. The middle classes who might have been expected to press for liberalisation, as their counterparts in Britain did for example, drew the lesson that any political alliance with the working class was dangerous because reform would lead to revolution. As a result, the middle classes tended to withdraw from politics leaving power firmly in the hands of the Austrian nobility. This only served to increase the resentment felt by the Italian and Hungarian nobles and the threat from these classes continued to be a major problem for the Monarchy in the coming years. More ominous still, the young Franz Joseph reasoned from the experience of 1848 that military force was the only way to ensure political stability and that any attempt to compromise or make concessions would lead to disaster. Hence the young Emperor rejected the radical Kremsier constitution offered by the Imperial parliament in January 1849 and reasserted the principle of one sovereign monarch answerable to no one but God and, of course, the Generals. In attaching the Monarchy so firmly to the army and the principles of absolutism Franz Joseph narrowed the range of political options open to him in the future to such an extent that it was virtually inevitable that the fate of the dynasty would be determined on the battlefield, as indeed it was. Thus, although little was achieved in 1848, the consequences of the revolutions were quite profound. The Monarchy had lost the goodwill of many of its subjects and because of this it faced the future after 1848, if not exactly doomed to destruction, with few clear political ideas other than a wish for survival.

Making notes on '*The Revolutions of 1848-9 in the Habsburg Empire*'

Although it is extremely important that you familiarise yourself with the course of events in 1848, it is equally vital not to spend too much time simply listing facts. You must concern yourself with the main issues and questions relating to this topic. However, this does not mean that you do not need to memorise the facts. The following questions are laid out in chronological order so that you should be able, as you answer the questions, to get a firm grasp of the issues and the events as they unfold. It would also help, at the end, to make a skeletal date chart just to strengthen your grasp of the factual outline.

1   What is the symbolic significance of Metternich's fall from power?
1.1 How important were the popular demonstrations in causing the fall of Metternich?
1.2 What was the role of court faction in Metternich's fall?
2   What were the April Laws?
3   Why was there a second revolution in Vienna?
4   What were the aims of the revolutionaries in Italy?
5   Why was the revolution defeated in Prague?
5.1 Why did the revolutions fail in Italy and Hungary?
6   What happened during the October Days?
7   What were the consequences of the failure of the revolutions within the Empire. Try to think in terms of both short- and long-term effects.

Answering essay questions on '*The Revolutions of 1848-9 in the Habsburg Empire*'

Essay questions on this period tend to fall into one of two categories. Firstly, there are those questions which focus on the causes of the revolutions. In this category the following are typical:

1   Why did Metternich fall from power?
2   What were the causes of the 1848 revolutions in the Habsburg Empire?
3   'The Revolutions of 1848 in the Habsburg Empire were almost entirely the result of discontent within the middle classes.' Discuss.

Perhaps the most sensible way to approach this type of question is to begin by trying to make a comprehensive list of all the reasons why the revolutions occurred. Simply list the factors to begin with: do not worry about the details. Having done this you will need to think carefully about how this list could be adapted to fit the specific questions. In what way, for example, does question 1 demand a different emphasis to that of question 2? Another useful task would be to try to put the various factors in order of relative importance. You may find this very hard to do because you are obviously dealing with more than one revolution. How will this affect the way you would plan essays 2 and 3 for example? Try drawing up an essay plan for question 2. You should find that the process of wrestling with the structure of an essay will help you focus your ideas.

The second sort of question deals with the reasons why the revolutions failed. Typical of this genre are:

4   Why did the 1848 revolutions in the Habsburg Empire fail?
5   Why did the Habsburg Monarchy survive the 1848 revolutions?
6   'In the end the bourgeoisie preferred order to liberty.' Discuss this verdict on the 1848 Revolutions in the Habsburg Empire.

Again, the obvious way to begin would be to make a list of the factors which led to the failure of the revolutions. You may find that each revolution demands a slightly different list. Is there one single dominant factor which holds true for all the failed revolutions? You must be careful to note the subtle differences between the questions. Question 5, for example, will require a little more knowledge about the actions of the court and the dynasty during the revolt. Finally you should be aware that questions on the 1848 revolutions often ask you to write about events in more than one country. For example, an interesting and challenging variant on the above question 5 would be:

7   Why did hereditary monarchy survive the 1848 revolutions in the Habsburg Empire and not in France?

This a very demanding question and one which requires information outside of the remit of this book. Obviously you need to relate what you have learned from this chapter to what you know about the 1848 revolutions in other parts of Europe.

Source-based questions on 'The Revolutions of 1848-9 in the Habsburg Empire'

1 The Role of the Middle Classes and the Nobility
Read carefully the extracts by Schwarzenberg and Metternich on page 56 and then answer the following questions:
a) What according to Schwarzenberg are the main weaknesses of the Austrian aristocracy? (2 marks)
b) How does Metternich's attitude to the Lombard aristocracy differ from Schwarzenberg's attitude to the Hungarian nobility? Why is there this difference? (8 marks)
c) Explain what Metternich means when he asks if the Lombard aristocracy want to 'surrender their fortunes on the high altar of some incredible divinity'. (5 marks)

2 The Role of Nationalism
Read carefully the extracts from Palacký and Mazzini on pages 57 and 58. Answer the following questions.
a) Who or what, according to Palacký, wishes to 'undermine Austria'? (2 marks)
b) Describe in your own words Palacký's attitude to the Empire. (4 marks)
c) What are the main differences between the nationalism preached by Palacký and that preached by Mazzini's followers? (9 marks)

3 The Suppression of the Revolutions
Study the cartoon on page 50 and answer the following questions.
a) Identify the aspects of this cartoon which suggest that the cartoonist was critical of these military leaders. (6 marks)
b) What do you consider to be the political message of this cartoon. (3 marks)
c) Imagine that you are a historian working on the 1848 revolutions. What are the strengths and weaknesses of this cartoon as a source? (6 marks).

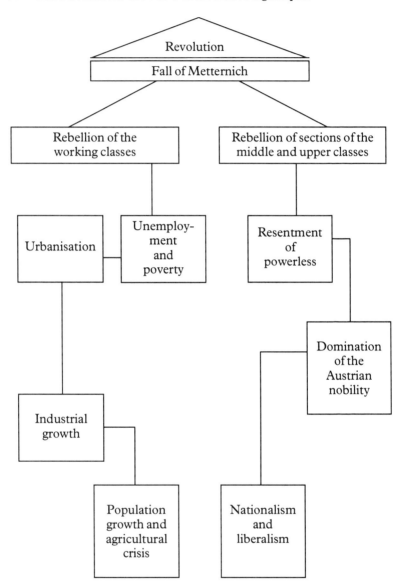

Summary - The Revolutions of 1848-9 in the Habsburg Empire

CHAPTER 4

The Search for Stability, 1848-67

1 Introduction

The history of the Habsburg Empire after the traumatic revolutions of 1848 is the history of a political system with an identity crisis. Constitutions came and constitutions went in a flurry of uncertainty. But, what does seem certain is that the identity crisis was resolved in 1867 when the old Austria of Metternich was finally buried and the new Austro-Hungarian Empire or Dual Monarchy was created as the result of the Emperor's Compromise (*Ausgleich*) with the Magyars. But exactly how was this personality change achieved?

The principal architect of the changes which restructured the Empire was the new young Emperor, Franz Joseph. However, it would be wrong to envisage a young man embarking coolly upon a series of political experiments. Instead, a man, old before his time, stumbled fitfully from one desperate gamble to another, pushed into domestic political change as often as not as a result of mistakes in foreign policy. Indeed, defeat in war was perhaps the principal catalyst for change in these years. It was war which destroyed Franz Joseph's attempts to return to absolutism after the revolutions of 1848, and it was war which forced him into the Compromise of 1867 which was to last until, fittingly, war destroyed it in 1918.

The purpose of this chapter is to examine and analyse the precise way in which old Austria was transformed into the Austro-Hungarian Empire and to assess whether or not that unintended development was, as is often claimed, a profound mistake.

2 Constitutional Change

a) Franz Joseph and the Return to Absolutism

By the end of the year 1848 it was still uncertain what kind of political settlement would emerge out of the chaos of revolution. The fighting was still going on in northern Italy and Hungary but, perhaps more importantly, the Imperial parliament was still in session at Kremsier, wherein the deputies sought to draft a new constitution. Although it was clear that the military leaders, Windischgraetz, Radetzky and Jellačič would eventually suppress the armed revolutionaries, there was still a hope amongst moderates that some sort of constitutional reform might be salvaged. It was this hope that inspired the deputies at Kremsier to continue working on their constitutional blueprint for a reformed Empire run largely by a central parliament with the power of the crown distinctly curtailed.

In hindsight it is easy to condemn the men of Kremsier as daydreamers. Certainly Windischgraetz was impatient and yearned to conclude their debates with cannon fire. But, by an odd quirk of history, it was Windischgraetz's brother-in-law, Prince Schwarzenberg, who insisted on subtler methods. Schwarzenberg was also prime minister and as such, given Franz Joseph's initial hesitancy, he was briefly the most powerful man in the Empire. Schwarzenberg's motives in restraining his brother-in-law and encouraging the Kremsier liberals and nationalists are open to debate. Some historians see his support for the Imperial parliament as a cynical deception but the weight of scholarship suggests that, although he had an unstable temperament, with a taste for violence and danger, he was, in his own rather hazy way, a believer in moderate constitutional reform. As soon as he was appointed prime minister in November 1848 he told the Imperial parliament that he wanted 'constitutional monarchy sincerely and unreservedly'. Schwarzenberg believed that some sort of constitutional reform was necessary because the aristocracy had proved itself incompetent as a governing elite: a working parliament was a way of by-passing the inept aristocracy and simultaneously creating a more unified, efficient and centralised Empire.

There is a touch of irony in this as Schwarzenberg came from one of the most illustrious aristocratic families in the Empire and in many ways embodied the faults of the arrogant and reckless aristocracy about which he was so concerned. His career record was littered with impetuous adventures, both political and amorous. As a young man he had self-consciously styled himself in the Byronic mould as a dashing gentleman with artistic sensibilities and a touching concern for the people. There is some evidence that he may have been quite radical in his younger days. For example, in 1825, while working as a diplomat in St. Petersburg, he had some rather shadowy involvement in the Decembrist Revolt of the Russian army officers against the Tsar. He also imitated Byron and indeed Prince Metternich in other ways. In London he had a notorious affair with the wife of the Lord Privy Seal and was only saved by the intervention of Metternich - who no doubt secretly approved of this application of the Metternichian method. But by 1848 Schwarzenberg no longer looked the part. He was 48 and his youthful good looks had withered after bouts of typhus fever. However, it was a great deal harder to tell if age had similarly withered his youthful idealism.

At first, Schwarzenberg moulded the Emperor to his own purposes. On the day after Franz Joseph's succession in December 1848, Schwarzenberg read out a Royal Address to the Kremsier Imperial parliament which seemed to suggest that the new Monarch was also in favour of constitutional Monarchy.

1 ... convinced, on our own motion, of the need and value of free
institutions expressive of the spirit of the age, we enter with due
confidence, on the path leading to a salutary transformation and
rejuvenation of the Monarchy as a whole. On the basis of genuine
5 liberty, on the basis of equality of all the nations of the realm and of
the equality before the law of all its citizens, and of participation of
those citizens in legislation, our Fatherland may enjoy a
resurrection to its old greatness and a new force. Determined to
maintain the splendour of the crown undimmed and the Monarchy
10 as a whole undiminished, but ready to share our rights with the
representatives of our peoples, we count on succeeding, with the
blessing of God and in understanding with our peoples, in uniting
all the regions and races of the Monarchy in one great state.

In fact the speech did not reflect Franz Joseph's views, only his
willingness, at this stage, to allow his prime minister to put words into
his mouth. However, the ideas of the Kremsier representatives soon
proved to be too radical for Schwarzenberg and he began to lose
patience. The fundamental sticking point was the question of
sovereignty. The deputies wished to assert the principle of popular
sovereignty: the idea that political power stems from the people and that
governments are therefore answerable to the people. Schwarzenberg,
although he was prepared to allow some limitations on the role of the
Monarch, remained attached to the notion that all sovereignty must
ultimately reside in the person of the Monarch rather than with the
people. In the final analysis, Schwarzenberg believed the people were
there to serve the Monarch, and not the other way round.

Franz Joseph it seems, despite his initial proclamation in favour of
constitutionalism, was, at heart, profoundly old-fashioned in his views.
He believed that a powerful Monarchy, answerable to no one except
God, was the only way to bind the disparate parts of his Empire
together. Thus the Kremsier constitution was unacceptable on a
philosophical basis even before the detail was worked out. The detail
that the Kremsier deputies finally came up with was in effect a suicide
note in the form of a constitution.

The Kremsier constitution was a model of radical liberal thought.
Theoretically, it would have left the crown without even a veto over
parliamentary legislation. It also sought to abolish the titles of the nobility
and to deprive the Roman Catholic Church of its status as the 'ruling'
religion. In addition to this came a long list of the 'Rights of Citizens',
including the equal value of the various languages of the citizenry. Only
in foreign policy was the crown given unrestricted authority.

At the beginning of March 1849 the men of Kremsier put forward
their liberal blueprint for Schwarzenberg's approval. To their
astonishment Schwarzenberg informed the representatives that the
Emperor had ignored their efforts and that a new constitution, drafted

by Count Stadion, the Minister of the Interior, would be issued for the Empire. On 4 March the so called Stadion Constitution was declared and the Kremsier parliament was quietly dissolved.

The Stadion Constitution was remarkably liberal in some ways. The Monarch was still to share power with an elected Imperial parliament, though he remained absolute in foreign policy. Many of the liberal Rights of Citizens were retained, as indeed was the principle of the equal value of all of the languages in the Empire. But even this more modest blueprint for reform was never put into operation. There are a number of reasons for this. Stadion, the minister who was responsible for the drafting of the constitution, was going slowly out of his mind, probably because of a syphilis infection. More critically, just at this point Schwarzenberg seems to have become anxious and uncertain about his political beliefs, whilst the young Franz Joseph seems to have grown in confidence and increasingly expressed his desire to rule as unlimited sovereign answerable only to God. In December 1849 the youthful Emperor remarked,

> The man who holds the reins of government in his hands must also be able to take responsibility. Irresponsible sovereignty are, for me, words without meaning; such a thing [limited monarchy] is a mere printing machine for signatures.

Though a young man, he had been brought up to think as old men thought. He was more at home with the ideas of Metternich than with the new liberal heresies, even at their most dilute. However, unlike Metternich, he was a serious and rather dull individual. Schwarzenberg's description of the young Emperor to Metternich is quite revealing.

1 The Emperor sees the magnitude and difficulty of his task and his will is firmly set to meeting it. His intelligence is acute, his diligence in business astonishing, especially at his age. He works hard for at least ten hours a day and no one knows better than I how many
5 ministerial proposals he sends back on the grounds of faultiness. His mien is dignified, his behaviour to everyone exceedingly polite though rather dry. Men of sentiment say he has not much heart. There is no trace in him of that warm superficial good-heartedness of many Archdukes, of the wish to please and make a personal
10 effect. On the other hand he is perfectly accessible, patient, and well disposed to be just to everyone.

Franz Joseph undoubtedly took his role extremely seriously. He wanted above all to see the Empire governed in a strong but fair way and yet he had a deep-seated distrust of politicians and an even deeper-seated respect for the power of the army. In large part this can be attributed to the fact that it was military might rather than political guile which effectively saved the dynasty in 1848. Indeed, he always retained a great sense of reverence for the army and he was regularly to be seen signing papers at his desk dressed in the uniform of a simple soldier in the Imperial army. He also took great pride in his status as Supreme Head of the armed forces.

There is one other important reason why the Stadion Constitution was never put into operation: the emergence of a new personality at court. Baron Kübeck was a politician of the old school. He was contemptuous of Schwarzenberg and Stadion and even more so of their flirtations with liberalism. He was a firm believer in the principle of absolutism. His uncomplicated message was, not surprisingly, seized upon by the earnest sovereign as the obvious solution to the Empire's current problems. Increasingly the Emperor turned to the obsequious Kübeck for advice, though he was apparently unaware that Schwarzenberg and Kübeck were great political rivals. Kübeck's policies were designed not only to be popular with the Emperor but also to frustrate the aims of Schwarzenberg. The Emperor was unwittingly at the centre of a ruthless power struggle. Extracts from Kübeck's diary give a flavour of the behind-the-scenes manoeuvring, and the manner in which Kübeck insinuated his way into the Emperor's favour.

1   9 January 1851 Call to the Emperor, who becomes more and more open. Great hopes in that fine young man! May they unfold successfully!

   19 January 1851 A change has come over my relation to the
5 Emperor. Prince Schwarzenberg's jealousy has been roused.

   3 June 1851 Pressure from the Emperor for political changes. My request for an interview.

   5 June 1851 Long conversation with the Emperor on our political situation. He asked me to put my proposals [for a return to
10 absolutism] on paper and send it to him. The Emperor seemed to be struck and went into everything in detail.

   23 June 1851 The Emperor, to whom I am called, is apprehensive of the possible resignation of Prince Schwarzenberg ... but declares that he is nevertheless determined on the step
15 advised.

   13 July 1851 Call to the Emperor. He tells me that he has read the work in question to Prince Schwarzenberg who stated his agreement with it. Prince Schwarzenberg does not dare to oppose the Emperor openly; he seeks to gain time to find ways and means
20 to upset the applecart.

By the end of 1851 it became clear that Schwarzenberg had lost the political struggle against Kübeck. Thus on 31 December 1851, after two years of what was in practice martial law, a new constitution was announced. It was known as the 'Sylvester Patent' (*Sylvesterabend* means New Year's Eve). The Patent re-established the absolute power of the Monarchy. Any existing checks on Franz Joseph's power were removed. An advisory council, known as the Reichsrat, was set up but it had no authority either to initiate or to block legislation. The role of ministers was reduced to that of officials receiving instructions from the Emperor.

If Kübeck felt that he had manipulated the Emperor he was wrong. In retrospect it is apparent that the strings were attached to the ambitious minister. Indeed, having served his purpose, Kübeck rapidly became irrelevant. Fortune also contributed to the Emperor's increased power. In 1852 both Count Stadion, the progressive Minister of the Interior, and Prince Schwarzenberg, perhaps the only man who ever briefly dominated Franz Joseph, died. Schwarzenberg's death coupled with the Sylvester Patent left the 20-year-old Emperor alone and absolute.

The Patent abolished almost all tiers of elected provincial and local government. The Empire was to be ruled from the centre. Austrian Law was declared the law of all the kingdoms, a development particularly resented in Hungary. The principle of linguistic equality was abolished along with a number of important liberal reforms such as the right to trial by jury, although the principle of equality before the new all-encompassing Imperial law was retained. The only major reform of 1848 to survive the backlash was the abolition of serfdom. Overall, the Sylvester Patent must be seen as something more than simply a return to the pre-revolutionary situation. The Patent created a more centralised and unitary constitution. It was in its own way a revolution: a 'revolution from above' ushering in a new absolutism.

b) Alexander Bach and the Consolidation of Absolutism

After Stadion's death Alexander Bach replaced him as Minister of the Interior. The period between the Sylvester Patent and the defeat at Solferino in 1859 (see page 74) is often known as the 'Bach era', largely because during this time Bach set about thoroughly reforming the administration of the Empire to create a more unitary state. Under Bach all claims to being a separate kingdom whether from Hungarians, Croatians or whoever were dismissed and the entire Empire was declared one centralised Imperial polity. Bach believed that the Empire should have one system of taxation, one internal market (the tariff border between Austria and Hungary was abolished by Bach in 1850), one system of law, one language for the authorities (German became the language of officialdom and was taught compulsorily in all secondary schools), and one system of overall administration. There should also be one body of uniformed German-speaking men to enforce this system. He was largely successful in introducing these reforms, though they were extremely unpopular with non-Germans and particularly with

Hungarians. The uniformed civil servants became known as 'Bach's Hussars' and provided a focus for hostility to the government.

In addition to this pattern of administrative uniformity, the state sought assistance from the Church to impose a uniformity of thought upon the masses. By the 1855 Concordat the Roman Catholic Church was given extensive rights over primary education, including a right to approve or disapprove of any teacher in a state school or university and the right to ban any book deemed unsuitable. In return for these concessions the Church inculcated loyalty and obedience to the Emperor. Thus the 'Bach era' must be seen as an emphatic reassertion of Habsburg authority in the wake of the failed revolutions of 1848. The forces which had prompted the 1848 uprisings, liberalism and nationalism, seemed entirely suppressed. But, in reality the edifice of this new absolutism was brittle and unstable. The strong winds of war turned it swiftly to political rubble.

3 War

Metternich's foreign policy had been based on the idea of a Concert of Powers holding together the European status quo, with the Habsburg Empire the necessary linchpin of that system. Towards the end of Metternich's time in office his grand system began to boil down to two basic ideas: in the east an unofficial alliance with Russia, and in the west continued domination of German affairs through the German Confederation. Between 1853 and 1866 Franz Joseph and his foreign ministers unintentionally undid the work of Metternich in both its main aspects.

a) The Crimea

Measured in terms of diplomatic consequences it can be said that the Crimean War was a war which the Habsburgs did not fight but which they still managed to lose.

What became the Crimean War began in 1853 when the Tsar sent his troops into the Turkish provinces of Wallachia and Moldavia in the Balkans on the pretext that he was defending the rights of Christians in that area. To the other great powers it appeared more like Russian expansionism. The British and French were determined to oppose this from the start, but Austria's position was more complex. On the one hand she valued her alliance with Russia - indeed Tsar Nicholas and Franz Joseph were great friends and in constant correspondence with one another - but on the other hand Russia could not be allowed to plunder the Balkan areas unrestrained. The Balkans naturally formed an area of strategic concern for the Habsburgs. Furthermore, if Russia was to accelerate the decline of Turkey, the so-called 'sick man of Europe', the consequences in terms of nationalist uprisings could be serious, and would probably also affect the Habsburg Empire. For these reasons Franz Joseph was determined to restrain the Tsar, though he hoped to avoid war.

At first Franz Joseph and his foreign minister Count Buol tried to act as mediators between the Russians and the Turks, but Tsar Nicholas was determined to push forward and on 1 October 1853 he declared war on Turkey. After five months of diplomatic wrangling Britain and France declared war on Russia. Franz Joseph and Buol were now forced to take sides or remain neutral. The Generals advised Franz Joseph to support Russia. The aged Metternich advised him to remain neutral. But Franz Joseph listened to his foreign minister who advised him to side with the west and seize this opportunity to assert himself in the Balkans. On 2 December 1854 Franz Joseph signed a treaty of alliance with France and Britain. This one act, it might be argued, created a tension between Russia and Austria in the Balkans that burned like the slowest of fuses until in 1914 it blasted both dynasties, and a great deal more besides, into historical oblivion.

There can be no doubt that Count Buol advised the young Emperor extremely unwisely. But Franz Joseph magnified the error by insisting that Habsburg armies remain mobilised but not actually at war. The net result of seeking to avoid giving offence, was, of course, to antagonise all parties. The Russians felt betrayed. Tsar Nicholas had died of stress during the war and his successor Alexander II openly heaped a share of the blame for Nicholas's death on Franz Joseph, and spoke menacingly of a future war if the Habsburgs did not change their course. The British were contemptuous of Austria's apparent faint-heartedness, and much more significantly the self-important Emperor of France, Napoleon III, who had somewhat bizarrely taken upon himself the role of liberator of Italy, became convinced that he could exploit Habsburg weakness to do something for the Italians under Habsburg rule. Ironically, although Habsburgs troops did not actually participate in the war, many thousands of them died as the result of the cholera epidemics which swept through the camps.

Italian nationalism was boosted by the Crimean War because, in contrast to the Empire, Piedmont, led by its prime minister Count Camillo Benso di Cavour, had fought alongside Britain and France with the result that Napoleon III became an unofficial supporter of the Piedmontese ambition to liberate northern Italy from Habsburg control and create a new major power. Napoleon III reasoned that such a new state would be a French ally and that he would emerge as an Italian liberator just as his more famous uncle had done years before. He judged that all this would be popular at home. Prussia, that other looming threat, had remained strictly neutral throughout the war thereby leaving herself complete diplomatic flexibility for the future. Bismarck was not as yet the Prussian chancellor, but there can be no doubt that he saw the germ of a future Prussian assault on Austrian hegemony in Germany inherent in Austria's friendless state.

Thus the Crimean War must be seen as a profound diplomatic defeat for Franz Joseph. Austria had lost the role which Metternich defined for it as the orchestrator of Europe's conservative powers. It had, in fact, alienated its principle ally, Russia, and ominously, the 'sick' condition of the Turkish Empire made future conflict in the Balkans almost inevitable.

b) France, Piedmont and Lombardy

After the Napoleonic wars and the settlement at Vienna in 1815 the Habsburgs had become, largely thanks to Metternich, the dominant power in Italian affairs. Italian nationalists regarded the Habsburgs as the main obstacle between them and the creation of an Italian nation state. In 1848-9 the Habsburgs successfully quelled the nationalists and Lombardy and Venetia seemed even more securely in the grip of the Empire. However, the diplomatic mistakes made over Crimea not only placed the Habsburgs in an isolated position, but they also inspired the state of Piedmont, the enemy in 1848, to challenge Habsburg dominance in northern Italy once again.

Piedmont's assault on Habsburg rule was masterminded by Cavour. Piedmont had fought, albeit rather ineffectively, in the Crimean War on the side of the French and British. As a result, Napoleon III began to regard Piedmont as an ally. This rather curious alliance was the primary reason why the Habsburgs were to lose their Italian possessions.

Napoleon III saw himself as a friend to Italian nationalists. As a younger man he had been a member of one the nationalist gangs known as the Carbonari. He felt, like many young men educated on the literature of ancient Rome, that the idea of an Italian nation was a noble and romantic one. More cynically, it could be argued that he saw the chance to extend French influence in Italy by backing Piedmont which then was likely to become a client state. This mixture of genuine emotional attachment to the cause combined with cool political calculation inclined Napoleon to support the cause of the Italian nationalists.

The nationalists responded by trying to assassinate him. In January 1858 Count Orsini, an unhinged Italian noble, hurled a bomb at Napoleon and his wife as they arrived at the opera. Napoleon survived but eight innocent people died. At his trial Orsini begged Napoleon to act upon his much vaunted nationalist beliefs. The French Emperor was moved by Orsini's eloquence. The Count was of course executed but Napoleon resolved to do something for Italy.

In July 1858 Napoleon met with Cavour at Plombières and promised that France would support Piedmont in a war with Austria so long as Austria was seen to be the cause of the war. Cavour thereupon set out to provoke the Austrians into war. He ordered his troops onto the border with Lombardy and made provocative speeches about the inadequacies of Habsburg rule. This should not have been enough for war. Cavour's plan seemed all but wrecked when the Tsar offered to mediate in an international peace conference to resolve the tension. But at this precise moment Count Buol decided that honour demanded that the Piedmontese be forced to back down. He sent an ultimatum to King Victor Emanuel demanding that his troops demobilise immediately. Unwittingly Buol had, in spite of dire warnings from Metternich, plunged the Empire into Cavour's trap. Piedmont refused, quite reasonably, to comply with the ultimatum and the result was war. France joined forces with Piedmont and after two decisive defeats in the summer of 1859 at Magenta and Solferino the Habsburgs were forced to agree to sign the peace of Villafranca which left Piedmont in control of Lombardy but not Venetia - much to Cavour's irritation. Nevertheless, Habsburg rule in northern Italy was dealt a fatal blow. Franz Joseph's instincts afterwards were to retreat from Italy. Count Buol was sacked and the loss of Venetia was just a matter of time.

4 Further Constitutional Change

a) The October Diploma, 1860

The defeats at Magenta and Solferino in 1859 gave ammunition to the liberal and nationalist critics of the existing absolutist constitution. But perhaps more disconcerting was the fact that European financiers refused to lend the Habsburgs any more money unless they introduced the kind of constitutional reforms which might appease the critics and thereby create a more stable political climate.

In order to buy off liberal discontent and rearrange the constitutional shop window more to the liking of Europe's bankers, the Emperor promised to modernise the institutions of the Empire. And yet he had not the slightest intention of liberalising the constitution. The idea of sharing power with a parliament or indeed trusting his people seemed to his mind more like an abdication. Nevertheless, something had to be done. In October 1860, acting on advice from the old conservative nobility, he announced a set of minor constitutional reforms collectively known as the October Diploma.

The intention behind the Diploma was to restore the influence of the aristocracy and to re-found the Monarchy upon a kind of federal basis in which the nobility were given considerable authority. In order to increase the power of the aristocracy, new provincial diets were set up as the instruments of aristocratic influence which would work in turn with an enlarged central Reichsrat (an advisory council of 100), in itself a return to an idea put forward by Metternich and later by Kübeck. The Emperor was required in theory to 'co-operate' with the diets and the

Reichsrat, and the latter had a right of veto over any new taxes. Thus to a small extent the Emperor's absolute power was curtailed. But the October Diploma lasted only four months. The reasons for its utter failure were numerous. Both the provincial diets and the central Reichrat lacked real power. Their 'co-operation' was in practice ordered by the Emperor. More fundamentally, the Emperor seems to have regarded the exercise as nothing more than a cynical piece of constitutional sleight of hand. He wrote to his mother when the October Diploma was issued, 'We shall indeed have a little parliamentary government, but the power remains in my hands'. In some ways the manner in which the constitution was created tells us more about the Emperor than the Diploma tells us about the Empire. Franz Joseph casually dictated the general principles on a train journey from Salzburg to Vienna. He then demanded of his bewildered ministers that a detailed constitutional document be produced in a week. The reason for this, it seems, is simply that he wanted to have some domestic success to boast of in order to impress his fellow monarchs, the Tsar of Russia and the King of Prussia, at a forthcoming meeting. As it turned out, neither the diplomatic summit nor the Diploma achieved anything.

However, the main reason for the failure of the Diploma was the response of the Hungarians. They demanded the recognition of the April Laws of 1848, which meant in practice a demand for almost complete self-government. Not only did they demand this, but they also refused to recognise the Diploma and carried out elections as if the April Laws were still in operation. Simultaneously they refused to send any representatives to Vienna. In short the October Diploma, hastily thrown together to stabilise the regime and boost the Emperor's flagging image, led instead to an embarrassing state of political anarchy.

b) The February Patent, 1861

Having dug himself into one hole, Franz Joseph appointed a new minister of state who promptly dug him into a different one. Anton von Schmerling was widely regarded as liberal because he had resigned in 1851 when the absolutist Sylvester Patent was issued. But this was a popular misconception. He had resigned because the Sylvester Patent diminished the authority of ministers such as himself. Politically, he was a believer in a centralised state dominated by Germans. His immediate task was to reverse the decentralising tendencies of the October Diploma whilst declaring that no such change was occurring and that the Diploma was, as the Emperor said, 'permanent and irrevocable'. For this reason Schmerling's new constitution introduced in 1861 and known as the February Patent was officially presented as an amendment to the October Diploma. However, in practice, Schmerling turned the October Diploma on its head, dropping federal ideas in favour of a return to centralisation. In essence, Schmerling increased the authority of the central Reichsrat and reduced the authority of the provincial diets. The latter were turned into electoral colleges for the purpose of selecting representatives for the Reichsrat which began to look like a parliament - and indeed is often referred to as one, although technically it was still only an advisory body and was still dominated by the nobility.

The new Reichsrat, which had an upper and a lower house, certainly had more authority than its predecessor. It could now initiate bills and was given a right of veto over all manner of domestic legislation. But its power was deliberately restricted in a number of important ways. Its ability to obstruct crown legislation was restricted by an 'emergency' clause which allowed the Emperor to make law when the parliament was not sitting. The crown also had the right to dissolve the parliament and to appoint ministers and the president and vice president of the Reichsrat. In addition, the crown could still rely on the support of the nobility in the upper house and in the lower house the balance of the nationalities was deliberately tipped in favour of Germans so that the possibilities of a nationalist revolt were negligible.

Again, perhaps the most significant weakness of the constitution was Franz Joseph's attitude to the Reichsrat. He saw it as at best an irrelevance, a necessary piece of hypocrisy. He made it quite clear that it would have no say in foreign affairs or in any military matters and it was precisely in these areas that the Emperor felt real power was located. Nevertheless, despite the tensions within Schmerling's repaired constitution, it survived until war in 1866 led to a new constitutional upheaval.

5 War: Prussia, Piedmont and Venetia

Franz Joseph recognised that 1859 effectively marked the end of the Habsburg mission in Italy and that the loss of Venetia was almost inevitable. At first the new Italian state based on Piedmont offered to purchase the province from the Habsburgs but Franz Joseph was too proud to consider selling his subjects for cash. His rejection of the offer had the effect of driving Italy into an alliance with Prussia, the latter now led by the bellicose prime minister Otto von Bismarck.

In Germany, Prussia had grown into a powerful industrial state and Bismarck was determined to challenge Austrian domination of German affairs. In 1866 the Empire was manoeuvred into a disastrous war by Bismarck, just as it had been seven years before by Cavour. Oddly enough in 1864 Austria and Prussia had been allies in a short, victorious war against Denmark, for which they were rewarded with the duchies of Schleswig and Holstein. In 1865 the two great powers agreed the so-called Convention of Gastein, which stipulated that Prussia was to administer Schleswig and Austria, Holstein. Once the agreement was made Bismarck sought to use it as a pretext for war, regularly claiming that Austria had broken the terms of the Convention. Franz Joseph grew angry but it was the Prussian proposal in 1866 to reform the constitution of the German Confederation in such a way as to exclude Austria entirely that finally prompted the Emperor to mobilise his armies for war.

Before actually declaring war the Habsburg Emperor sought to make sure that France would remain neutral. So great was the threat from Prussia that Franz Joseph decided to cede Venetia to France, to be passed on to Italy, in return for French neutrality and the promise that France would do her best to keep Italy neutral. Napoleon III agreed to this, perhaps relishing the prospect of two great rivals preparing to exhaust each other in a long and bloody war.

The illogicality of the situation the Emperor had manoeuvred himself into has baffled many students of the period. His refusal to sell Venetia had made an enemy of Italy, which was now determined to fight alongside Prussia. Thus he had created a situation in which Habsburg armies in northern Italy found themselves fighting to retain a territory that their Emperor had secretly decided, win or lose, to give away. But the situation was not perhaps as paradoxical as it seems because it was clear that to ensure continued French neutrality Venetia had to be retained until the end of the war. And, of course, the most satisfactory overall explanation is that by 1866 the Emperor had come to see the defeat of Prussia as the number one priority: as something infinitely more important than the retention of a corner of northern Italy.

Franz Joseph genuinely believed that French neutrality would tip the balance in favour of the Habsburg armies. He was wrong. Instead, the Imperial armies suffered a crushing defeat at the hands of the Prussian at the battle of Sadowa (Königgrätz) on 3 July 1866. The resulting peace agreement, the Treaty of Prague, effectively ejected Austria from German affairs. The German Confederation was abolished and a new political entity emerged, consisting of all but the southern German states, known as the North German Confederation and dominated by Prussia. It is common to ascribe the end of 400 years of Habsburg authority in Germany to the superior firing rate of the Prussian needle-gun (the first efficient breech-loading rifle). It is not so commonly known that the Austrian government, only a few years before Sadowa, had decided not to adopt the needle-gun because it was too expensive. In the end it was, perhaps, Prussian economic strength which told.

Ironically, Austrian forces in Venetia rapidly defeated the Italian forces but the province was still duly given to Napoleon III, who was thus able to fulfil his self-appointed role as the liberator of Italy and deliver it to his defeated ally. As a result of Sadowa the Habsburgs found themselves pushed out of both Germany and Italy. The Empire had lost its traditional spheres of influence, and not surprisingly the foreign crisis generated a domestic crisis with its own important consequences.

6 The Last Constitutional Change

Defeat at Sadowa, as at Solferino seven years earlier, proved to be an important catalyst for domestic political change. The reasons for this are not hard to find. By 1866 the identity crisis had become acute. In terms of foreign policy, the Habsburgs had been ejected from the traditional spheres of influence carved out for them by Metternich in 1815 and they remained diplomatically isolated. At home, news of the triumphs of German and Italian nationalism reactivated the nationalist movement, which in turn led to calls for the abolition of Schmerling's constitution which centralised power in Vienna and tended to favour Germans. The Magyars, in particular, resented the way in which the February Patent refused to recognise their rights as a distinct kingdom. Not surprisingly, Hungarian nationalists sought to exploit the crisis to press their claims for a return to the April Laws of 1848. However, at this juncture, with Kossuth still in exile, radical or separatist nationalism was a relatively weak political force. The leadership of the nationalist cause had passed into the hands of Francis Deák, a more moderate, some would say realistic, leader than Kossuth. Deák realised that Hungary could not, at this time, hope to break away from Austria, but thought that some sort of compromise could still be sought which would increase the measure of self-government she enjoyed.

A year before the crisis brought about by Sadowa occurred, Deák had, in a series of newspaper articles, defined his vision of a 'Dual Monarchy' in which Hungary would be given the status of an autonomous kingdom which nevertheless recognised a Habsburg as their legitimate sovereign. Franz Joseph was impressed by Deák's loyalty, although he was less happy with his refusal to allow Hungarian representatives to attend Schmerling's central Reichsrat. The Hungarians had killed the October Diploma by simply refusing to recognise its existence and now, led by Deák, they were once again steadily undermining the constitutional basis of the Empire. The Emperor might shrug off Hungarian non co-operation in ordinary circumstances but in times of war he found himself uncomfortably dependent upon Hungarian goodwill. In particular, after the defeat at the hands of Bismarck's armies at Sadowa, Franz Joseph was forced to recognise that if he was to have revenge, inevitably he would need Hungarian military support. Deák, though a reasonable and polite man, made it clear that the price of Hungarian support was the adoption of his Dualist constitution.

The Emperor's delusions of revenge were undoubtedly a powerful motive for accepting Deák's package. But he rather resented the way his hand was being forced. He might never have agreed to Deák's terms had it not been for the fact that Deák sent a particularly persuasive minister to negotiate with him. Count Julius Andrássy was a dashing Hungarian noble with a talent for diplomacy. In the weeks after Sadowa he travelled to Vienna to discuss proposals for constitutional reform with Franz Joseph. Andrássy's impact upon the Emperor was made all the greater by the fact that he seems to have rapidly become the favourite of the Empress Elizabeth. The Empress was at this point in her life recovering from anorexia nervosa and was still emotionally very fragile. Dazzled as she was by Andrássy, she urged her husband to accept the Hungarian plans and he did not wish to upset her.

The promptings of his wife and the desire for some sort of revenge led Franz Joseph to sit down with Andrássy to discuss the detail of Deák's proposals. He became convinced that a compromise with the Hungarians might be a way of renewing the strength and vitality of the Empire. However, he was also aware that any concessions to the Hungarians would meet with powerful political resistance from the Austrian Germans in the Reichsrat. In order to get around this, in an extraordinary move, Franz Joseph brought in an outsider, Baron Friedrich von Beust, the foreign minister of Saxony, as a new Minister President with the responsibility for creating a new constitutional arrangement along Dualist lines. Beust worked well with Andrassy. In order to defeat their political opponents in the Reichsrat they ruthlessly exploited the possibilites in the February Patent for dictatorial government. The various laws which made up the Compromise were simply set in front of the Reichsrat as a *fait accompli*. The Reichsrat had no choice but to vote for them or find itself dissolved. In 1867 the Compromise or *Ausgleich* was made law.

7 The *Ausgleich*

a) The Terms of the Settlement

The so-called Compromise was exactly that. It allowed the Hungarians a considerable measure of control over their domestic affairs but simultaneously forced them to recognise, in theory at least, that they were still part of a greater and indivisible Imperial entity. Thus with remarkable sleight of hand the Empire was both divided and unified. It was divided in that the lands to the east of the small river Leitha (known as Transleithania), including not only Hungary but also Transylvania and Slovakia - Croatia enjoyed a peculiar semi-autonomous status, although clearly inferior in terms of political significance within the Empire - were now under the authority of the parliament at Budapest, whilst the western half of the Empire (known as Cisleithania) fell under the jurisdiction of the Reichsrat in Vienna, now raised to the full status of a parliament. In all domestic matters the two parliaments functioned independently of each other. To emphasise the new duality Franz Joseph was known as both Emperor of Austria and King of Hungary and because of this the Empire after 1867 was referred to either as the Dual Monarchy or the Austro-Hungarian Empire.

However, although the agreement in many ways increased the rights of the Magyars, the Compromise was also designed to bind Hungary firmly to the Habsburgs. The package of legislation that comprised the settlement specified that as far as foreign and military affairs were concerned the Dual Monarchy was one entity. Hence the settlement stipulated that there would be one Imperial army and three common ministries - foreign affairs, defence (war), and finance. The Emperor retained control over the appointments to these ministries and in particular over the post of minister for foreign affairs which became a prime ministerial position. There was also a common customs union, although this was to be renegotiated very 10 years.

Clearly such an arrangement necessitated some degree of common taxation. The so-called tax quota proved to be a highly contentious issue not only in 1867 but over the next 50 years. Nevertheless the relative revenue contributions of the Austrian and Hungarian halves of the Empire were set at 70 per cent and 30 per cent respectively. This fiscal concession to the Magyars was the price that Franz Joseph was prepared to pay for the preservation of his own power.

b) Assessing the *Ausgleich*

The agreement can be criticised on the grounds that it was imposed on the peoples of the Empire without consultation. The Slavs, such as the Croats, now placed under Magyar rule, were fiercely hostile to the settlement because they felt it would diminish their own authority in the province of Croatia. Even some Hungarians resented it. Kossuth, the exiled Hungarian hero of 1848, denounced the Compromise as insufficient. But this is perhaps a rather weak line of criticism. Most decisions taken by almost any government anywhere in nineteenth century Europe were imposed on the people without consultation and the fact that the Compromise was unpopular with most subjects in the Empire does not necessarily mean that it was doomed to fail.

A slightly stronger argument would be that the Compromise introduced a large element of constitutional confusion. Austrians tended to assume that there was still a unitary state, within which there were two halves, but Hungarians saw themselves as living in an almost independent state which just happened to share a sovereign with its neighbour. The ambiguity about the exact nature of Dualism was inevitably a source of tension.

More positively it could be argued that a degree of constitutional imprecision provided the necessary flexibility for the agreement to work. So long as neither partner forced the issue it was perfectly possible perhaps for serene confusion to lubricate the settlement.

But it might still be claimed that issues were bound, from time to time, to be forced. For example, the Magyars were determined to have their own army but Franz Joseph insisted that there be only one

Imperial-royal army with German as the official language of command. The Magyars bitterly resented this state of affairs but could not alter the Emperor's mind. However, in a fudge that typifies the nature of the entire Compromise the Hungarians were allowed a small home defence force which Andrássy immediately labelled the Hungarian national army (Honvédseg). Although this issue continued to be a highly contentious one right up the outbreak of the Great War it is worth noting that Hungarian troops remained loyal to the Empire throughout almost the entire course of the war. There were of course numerous other sources of friction. The quota of taxes to be paid to Vienna was a constant source of friction but never enough to threaten the stability of the Dualist system.

Economically, the *Ausgleich* has also been evaluated in differing ways. It used to be thought that it worked to the economic advantage of the Austrians and that the Hungarian half of the Monarchy became in effect an internal colony, ruthlessly exploited by Austrian capitalists looking for under-developed economies which might provide a quick return on their capital. Hence Austrian entrepreneurs could be said to have milked Hungary for fast returns without due consideration for the national good of Hungary. It is also true that the export of Hungarian agriculture provided much of the finance for the purchase of materials necessary to Austrian industrialisation. If this is true it can be argued that the dependent position Hungary entered into actually retarded her development and enforced a condition of backwardness. However, all of this is highly debatable. David Good argues, in *The Economic Rise of the Habsburg Empire,* that in fact the relationship was mutually advantageous. Gradually the Empire became a much more integrated economic unit and the growth rates were at least average by European standards. In fact, between 1870 and 1913 the economic growth rate in the entire Habsburg Empire, according to Good, was fractionally better than that of the British economy. If Good's revisionism is correct, it may be fair to conclude that the *Ausgleich* was a success economically.

Finally, and most dramatically, it is sometimes argued that the Compromise gave the Magyars effective control over any future political developments within the Empire. This was certainly true in that the agreement gave the Magyars a veto over any subsequent constitutional change. However, the real significance of this point is that the Compromise with the Magyars seemed effectively to close off any chance of a similar Compromise with the Slavs. The Magyars were a minority even in their half of the Empire and they were determined not to share power with Slavs, such as their main rivals the Croats. Magyar policy toward the various Slav groups was based on a simple determination to dominate them and most importantly to block any concessions the Habsburgs might wish to make to them. Given that Slav nationalism was to grow strong in the second half of the nineteenth century, the fact that the *Ausgleich* prevented the Habsburgs appeasing the Slavs or adapting the constitution to give them greater rights would seem to be of great significance. Furthermore, if we remember that it was the problem of Slav nationalism which precipitated the war which eventually destroyed the Empire it is indeed possible to see the Habsburgs in 1867 entering not simply into an alliance but into a fatal embrace.

The logic of this argument seems impressive, but do the facts support the idea that the Magyars should be blamed for leading the Habsburg Empire to its doom? It would certainly seem that the Hungarians became very powerful as a result of the Compromise. The settlement meant that the Magyars effectively governed slightly over half of the Habsburg lands, despite making up only one fifth of the population. They had been handed a kind of legal and racial supremacy over the Slavs in the east of the Empire. Indeed the Compromise confirmed the Magyars in their self-image as one of the two 'master races' ruling over the racially and culturally inferior Slavs. The tone of this new and slightly sinister racial alliance is captured in Andrássy's apocryphal instruction to Franz Joseph, 'You take care of your Slavs and we will take care of ours'.

The Magyars did indeed take a great deal of care in their attempts to obliterate the Slavs culturally. Not only did they oppress and abuse the Slav nationalities, but they also sought to force them to give up their ethnic identity and become Hungarian. This policy is usually referred to as Magyarisation. The main instrument of Magyarisation was education policy: between 1879 and 1907 they passed a series of laws which made Hungarian the compulsory language of instruction in most schools and in some cases they actually closed down Slav secondary schools on the grounds that they were promoting the 'backward' culture of the Slavs and encouraging resistance to the 'superior' culture of the Magyars. The policy stretched wider than mere education. Place names were Magyarised. Local cemeteries were instructed to Magyarise the names of the dead for the headstones. The Press was tightly controlled and dissidents found themselves on trial for subversive activities. All of this was made possible because of the way in which the Magyars had arranged the electoral system so as to disenfranchise the vast majority of non-Magyars.

However, no matter how much we dislike reading about such unpleasant policies we must not allow out distaste to colour our judgements. Did the policy of Magyarisation destabilise the Empire? The answer, according to Alan Sked's survey of recent research in *The Decline and Fall of the Habsburg Empire, 1815-1918*, would seem to be, 'No'. Despite the awful repressiveness of the regime there was little serious opposition. In fact, in some ways it was a very successful policy. Large numbers of the German-speaking middle and upper classes transformed their identity into something suitably Magyar. The Jewish community also rapidly assimilated themselves into the official culture.

Indeed, anyone with ambition inevitably learnt the language and adopted the outlook of the Magyars. Only in the politically powerless outlying rural villages of Slovakia, Ruthenia and the South Slav lands did the Magyarisation policy fail to make much impact. But semi-literate peasants were no threat to the *Ausgleich*. Indeed, revisionist historians have pointed out the lack of organised opposition to the Magyars in their half of the Empire. Furthermore, it must always be remembered that no matter how much power the Magyars appeared to have, in the last resort the Emperor could, if he so chose, overrule the Budapest parliament in his role as their sovereign. In short, we must be careful before heaping the blame for the eventual dissolution of the Empire on the Hungarians and on the Compromise of 1867. In Alan Sked's words,

> there can be no case for arguing that by 1914 the Hungarians had brought the Monarchy to the brink of dissolution on account of their treatment of the nationalities, however unjust it may have been.

In conclusion then, although the *Ausgleich* clearly had its faults and may have limited the room for manoeuvre that Franz Joseph had in subsequent years, it did have one great strength: it put an end to the cycle of constitutional change. In that sense it was an unexpected solution to the identity crisis that followed the revolutions of 1848.

Making notes on 'The Search for Stability, 1848-67'

The main problem facing any student of this era in the history of the Habsburg Empire is undoubtedly the rather bewildering turnover of constitutions. Because of this it would probably be wise to write a brief description of each constitution up to and including the *Ausgleich*. You should also make notes on the foreign policy developments in these years. You may find these headings useful:

1   The Kremsier Constitution, 1849. Note the many points and why it failed.
1.1 The Stadion Constitution, 1849. Why did it fail to be implemented?
2   The Sylvester Patent, 1851.
3   The October Diploma, 1860.
3.1 The February Patent, 1861.
4   The *Ausgleich*, 1867. Carefully note the terms of this successful constitution. Explain how and why it came about.
5   How did the Crimean War affect the Habsburg Empire?
6   Loss of territory in Italy. Explain the reasons why the Habsburgs lost Lombardy and Venetia.
7   War against Prussia. Why did the Empire go to war with Prussia?
7.1 What were the consequences of defeat?

8   How have historians differed in their assessment of the *Ausgleich?*

Answering essay questions on 'The Search for Stability, 1848-67'

The majority of questions on the Habsburg Empire in this period focus on two issues: internal changes culminating in the *Ausgleich*, and foreign policy problems. The following are fairly typical of the first variety:

1   How effective were Franz Joseph's domestic policies in the period between 1848 and 1867?
2   Explain why there was so much constitutional change in the Habsburg Empire between 1848 and 1867.

Clearly in both cases it is important that you are able to explain why there was so much constitutional upheaval in this period. Make an essay plan for one of these two questions. Having done that, try to write a short, emphatic concluding paragraph.

The second sort of question is primarily about foreign policy, such as:

3   Assess Franz Joseph's conduct of Habsburg Foreign policy between 1848 and 1867.
4   Explain why the Habsburg Empire suffered defeats in Germany and Italy between 1849 and 1867.

Both of these questions require a detailed understanding of the twists and turns in international relations during this period. One way of dealing with these questions is to focus on the aims of the Emperor. Question 4 requires a factoral approach - you must try to avoid narrating the story of Austrian foreign policy. Make a list of factors involved in the failure of foreign policy in these years.

Finally you should be aware that questions on the Habsburgs can often be subsumed into wider questions on Italian or German Unification. If you intend to prepare for these topics you will need to look at *The Unification of Germany* and *The Unification of Italy*, both by Andrina Stiles in this series.

Source-based questions on 'The Search for Stability, 1848-67'

1 Franz Joseph and the Kremsier Constitution
Carefully read Schwarzenberg's 'Royal Address' to the Kremsier deputies on page 66-7 and Franz Joseph's remarks in December 1849 on page 68. Answer the following questions.
a)   Explain which phrases in the Royal Address would have pleased the Kremsier liberals and why. (5 marks)
b)   Compare the Royal Address with the remarks of December 1849.

What do these sources suggest about the young Emperor's changing political attitudes? (6 marks)

c) How reliable is the Royal Address as a guide to Franz Joseph's future intentions? (4 marks)

2 The Diary of Kübeck

Carefully read the extracts from Kübeck's diary on page 69. Answer the following questions:

a) Explain what Kübeck meant when he wrote that the Emperor was 'determined on the step advised'. (3 marks)

b) What does Kübeck's diary suggest about the author's aims and intentions? (7 marks)

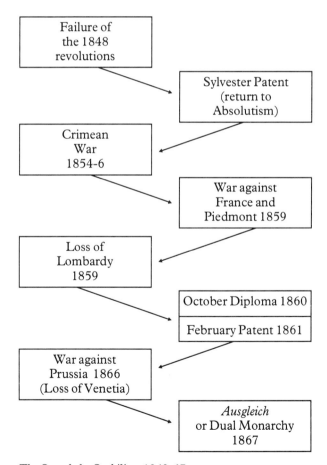

Summary - The Search for Stability, 1848-67

CHAPTER 5

The Habsburg Empire, 1867-1914

1 Domestic Politics

Before embarking upon a description of the political events in the Habsburg Empire between 1867 and 1914 it is best to pause to consider the nature of the political system. But this raises a major problem: it was not one political system, but two distinct systems, one centred on Vienna and the other in Budapest. There may have been a certain outward appearance of unity, given that the Emperor did have effective control over foreign policy, and no doubt the lives of the peasantry seemed much the same on either side of the Leitha - the stream which divided the two halves of the Empire - but domestically the two halves of the Empire led very different political lives.

In the Austrian half (Cisleithania) there was a fitful move towards democracy, eventually embracing universal suffrage. In the Hungarian half (Transleithania) the Magyars refused to countenance such changes, with the result that the *Ausgleich* was placed under increasing stresses and strains. But it would be wrong to imagine that the western half was therefore liberal and progressive whilst the eastern half was crudely reactionary. In a very real sense the contradictory policies were simply different solutions to the same problem, namely the rise of nationalism. The second half of the nineteenth century saw a rapid spread of nationalist feeling right across Europe. Obviously in a state that embraced at least eleven different national groups, this was a very dangerous phenomenon. In many respects then the story of domestic politics within the Empire up to 1914 can very largely, but not quite entirely, be seen as the struggle to contain and assimilate the energies of the nationalists.

a) The Complexity of the Nationalities Problem

Most historians would agree that the key to unlocking the mysteries of the Habsburg Empire is an understanding of the complexity of the nationalities question. But, in some ways, the situation was straightforward. The Habsburg Empire was a vast multinational state within which there were, after 1867, two dominant racial groups: the Germans and the Magyars, each ruling over their respective half of the Empire. But it would be wrong simply to lump all the other nationalities together as an equally oppressed, second-class mass. Within the Dualist structure some of the lesser national groups were in a more favoured situation. In fact, there existed a curious kind of dualism within dualism. In each half of the Empire the ruling nationality had allowed one Slav group to establish for itself considerable rights of self-government. In Cisleithania the Poles had been allowed to govern the large province of Galicia almost entirely as they wished, much to the annoyance of the Ruthenians who lived among them. In Transleithania the Croats established very significant rights of self-government for the province of Croatia-Slavonia.

Beneath the Croats and the Poles the various other, predominantly Slav, groups had little power and very little unity of purpose. Groups such as the Slovenes, the Slovaks and the Romanians were primarily peasant peoples with little interest in abstract ideas such as nationalism. Peoples marked out by their religion, such as the Jews or the Moslems in Bosnia spent most of their time trying to disguise their difference and blend into Habsburg society. There were perhaps only two groups with serious aspirations to break away from the Empire - the Italians and the Serbs. In both cases this was partly because there existed an independent state outside of the Empire into which these people hoped to be assimilated. After the establishment of an independent Italy in 1860, the Italians of the south Tyrol and the Adriatic coastline began to look to it for liberation. But the Italians were few in number and the Italian state showed little interest in them and indeed remained an ally of the Habsburgs until 1915 (when the western allies secretly offered Italy Habsburg Italian provinces as a bribe to bring Italy into the war against Austria-Hungary). The Serbs in the Balkans looked to the neighbouring independent state of Serbia as their natural homeland. However, although it was the Serbian question which precipitated the Great War in 1914, before the turn of the century neither the Serbs nor the Italians presented a great threat to the stability of the Empire. Indeed, the only national group within Cisleithania which seemed capable of seriously agitating for change before 1900 was the Czechs and for that reason the Czech question is undoubtedly the main theme in Austrian domestic politics in the nineteenth century. In Transleithania the policy of Magyarisation, for all its faults, seemed to keep the lid firmly on the nationality question.

b) Nationalism in Cisleithania

To the west of the river Leitha the most divisive political issue after 1867 was the so-called Czech question. Throughout the period between the *Ausgleich* and the outbreak of the Great War there was considerable tension between the dominant Germans and the Czechs. The latter resented being ruled over by Germans and the fact that German was the language of officialdom even in predominantly Czech areas. The problem was made more acute by the fact that, although the Germans were the largest single group in Cisleithania (36 per cent in 1880), the Czechs were not only the second largest ethnic group (23 per cent), but were also the majority in their 'historic' homelands of Bohemia and Moravia. The census of 1900 reveals the extent to which the Czechs were in the numerical majority there.

The nationalities of the Czech lands in 1900			
	Czechs	Germans	Others
	%	%	%
Bohemia	62.68	37.26	0.06
Moravia	71.36	27.90	0.74

Not surprisingly, with such a numerical advantage the Czechs began to press for greater rights. In many ways the problem can simply be presented as a constitutional question. After all, the Czechs most emphatically did not want independence. They simply wanted a measure of autonomy for Bohemia and Moravia within an Imperial framework.

i) The Roots of the Czech Question

However, although the conflict at the political level often did focus on constitutional rights, the catalyst for change was in practice the rapid socio-economic and cultural changes that occurred in Bohemia and Moravia in the second half of the nineteenth century. Underpinning the changing aspirations of the Czech people, and perhaps setting them apart from the more politically dormant Slav peoples elsewhere in the Empire, was the great industrial strength of Bohemia. In the first half of the century Bohemia had already established itself as the centre of the Empire's textile industry, but in the 1860s the Bohemian economy also became the focus of a rapidly expanding heavy engineering industry. The jewel in the crown of this new industrialisation was the Skoda works at Pilsen, which soon became the source of most of the Empire's armaments.

The social effects of Bohemia's industrial revolution were equally marked. Czechs found themselves attracted away from the land and into the towns. The city of Prague, for example, which had been predominantly German at the start of the century, was 94 per cent Czech by 1910. Furthermore, many Czech businessmen made a lot of money. By the time of the *Ausgleich* there existed a Bohemian bourgeoisie which had economic but not political power. The latter remained in German and Magyar hands. The discontents of the Czech bourgeoisie provided the motor for the Czech nationalist movement.

In addition to the social changes, there were very significant cultural shifts occurring in the Czech lands which were equally as important in shaping the subsequent development of the Czech question. As early as 1836 the great nationalist Jan Palacký had written a *History of the Bohemian People,* published in the Czech language, which helped to encourage national pride. In effect Palacký's history began the slow process of awakening the Czech people to their own past. But his writings were also in their own way a form of political propaganda. His books were largely responsible for turning many ordinary Czech men and women into nationalists. Later in the century other cultural developments continued Palacký's work. In 1881 the Bohemian Theatre opened, putting on plays in Czech rather than German, and in 1882 a specifically Czech university was established in Prague. This combination of socio-economic and cultural change eventually gave rise to a nationalistic political party, the Young Czechs, which pressed both for constitutional change and greater civil rights for Czech-speaking people.

ii) The Politics of the Czech Question

There can be little doubt that Franz Joseph's Compromise with the Hungarians in 1867 produced considerable resentment in Bohemia and Moravia. Many Czech nationalists simply refused to recognise the legitimacy of the new constitution. This led rapidly to a decision to boycott the central Reichsrat in Vienna altogether. The Emperor sought ways of appeasing them, largely because he had no wish to see moderate Czech nationalist feeling turn into something more extreme. In 1871 the Emperor and his prime minister, Count Hohenwart, negotiated a series of what were in effect radical amendments to the *Ausgleich,* which the Czechs were willing to accept. The most significant part of Hohenwart's proposals was the idea that Bohemia and Moravia would be governed by a parliament in Prague and that on all purely domestic issues this parliament would be sovereign. But the Emperor was not ready for the storm of opposition that these proposals provoked. The Germans in Bohemia and Moravia protested. German students in Vienna rioted. Leaders of the army and the Civil Service expressed their concern that this would weaken the Empire. But the crucial opposition came from Hungary. Andrássy, now Hungarian Minister President, called it a violation of the *Ausgleich* and reputedly asked Hohenwart if he was ready to carry through the policy with cannon. In the event Andrássy's words were all the firepower necessary. Forced to choose between the Magyars and the Czechs, Franz Joseph sided with the former and the Hohenwart proposals were shelved, permanently as it turned out.

Despite this disappointment for Czech nationalists, the Czech question continued to be the key to Austrian politics. There are perhaps two reasons why this was so. First, Czech nationalism was a growing movement with a considerable momentum of its own: a momentum only increased by the anger inspired at the sudden collapse of the Hohenwart proposals. Secondly, more subtly, the Czechs came to be seen by the Emperor as a vital ally in the struggle against what Franz Joseph saw as a more corrosive force, German Liberalism.

Ever since 1867 Austrian politics had been dominated by the German Liberals. From the Emperor's perspective this was to be lamented. The

Liberals passed legislation which could be said to have undermined the traditional basis of royal authority. The Liberal Party was anti-clerical; it revoked the Concordat of 1855 which had given the Catholic Church considerable influence in all areas of civil society. The Church's monopoly on education and marriage services was also broken. Furthermore the Liberals, being predominantly bourgeois, tended to pass free trade legislation and weaken the traditional position of the landed classes in Austrian society. Both of these trends were bitterly resented by Franz Joseph. But above all he opposed the Liberal belief that the Emperor should be made more responsible to parliament. Liberals wanted to see the influence of the Monarchy reduced. This condition of mutual suspicion reached a head in 1878 when the Liberals opposed Franz Joseph's decision to annex Bosnia and Herzegovina. This was to prove a turning point. The Liberals fell from power and Franz Joseph cast around for a way of preventing them from ever forming another government. The Czechs were part of his solution.

Franz Joseph's first move against the Liberals was to appoint an old friend, Count Taaffe, as prime minister. Taaffe was committed to the idea that the Empire should not be dominated by any one party. To this end he set about putting together a coalition of groups which would support the Emperor and consequently keep the German Liberal Party out of office. The support of the representatives of the landed classes, known as the 'Feudals', was relatively easy to obtain. The party of the Catholic Church, the so-called Clericals, was also quick to join an anti-Liberal bloc. But Taaffe realised that he would need the support of certain Slav groups if the German Liberals were to be effectively excluded. The Poles were already loyal, given the considerable amount of autonomy they enjoyed in Galicia. The Czechs were the vital last piece of the jigsaw puzzle. In 1879 they were still boycotting the central parliament. Their support would have to be bought.

Suddenly the government was falling over itself to offer concessions to the Czechs. In 1880 Taaffe successfully introduced legislation which established that government officials in Bohemia and Moravia must use the Czech language when dealing with Czech people. This was a symbolic triumph won in the teeth of a great deal of German opposition. In 1882 Taaffe granted official recognition to the Czech University in Prague. The result of these concessions was that the Czechs became, temporarily at least, partners in a political coaliton of Feudals, Clericals and Slavs which contemporaries dubbed the 'Iron Ring'.

Historians have tended to be fairly critical of the Iron Ring, seeing it as a kind of quick fix which offered no long-term solutions to the Monarchy's problems. Indeed Count Taaffe admitted that his only guiding principle in these years was that of 'muddling through' *(fortwursteln)*. It is therefore hard to resist the notion that the Iron Ring was almost bound to come apart. Having given concessions to the Young Czechs it was inevitable that they would want more. It soon became evident that the Iron Ring not only excluded the Liberals but also encircled and entrapped Count Taaffe.

In 1893 Taaffe sought to weaken the power of the Young Czech party in Bohemia and Moravia by extending the franchise to the working classes, who were thought to be rather more interested in improving their working conditions than in nationalist agitations. But the Ring was a deeply traditonal, conservative alliance and was profoundly hostile to radical ideas such as democracy. Taaffe's bill was voted down and he fell from office, having been in effect devoured by a monster of his own making. He had sought to use the Young Czech party but, instead, it had used him and had grown stronger in the process.

After the fall of Taaffe and the disintegration of the Iron Ring, Franz Joseph increasingly came to regard the Reichsrat as a virtually uncontrollable collection of squabbling factions. Nationalism had grown to such an extent that it was almost impossible to do anything without some national group objecting. The government that immediately followed Taaffe was brought down by the Slovenes demanding similar language rights to that of the Czechs. The Czechs for their part, whilst agreeing with the Slovenes, wanted greater linguistic rights for themselves. Indeed, it was the issue of the Czech language which was to reduce the Reichsrat to the level of pure farce and to push Franz Joseph to the most desperate of measures.

The crisis came to its height during the Badeni ministry of 1895-7. In many ways the cause of the crisis might be thought a relatively trivial issue. Count Badeni, the prime minister, attempted to win the support of the Czechs in the Reichsrat by offering to modify Taaffe's original concessions on the language question in such a way that it would become compulsory for all civil servants in Bohemia and Moravia to become bilingual. But Badeni had underestimated the strength of German resistance to such a measure. Germans had always regarded the Empire as primarily a Germanic entity and themselves as essentially the dominant race within it. But in 1896 Badeni, himself a Pole, had reformed the franchise in such a way as to diminish the number of German representatives and to slightly increase the number of Slavs. As a result the Germans were in no mood to grant any further concessions in 1897. When Badeni brought forward his Czech language bill in 1897 the German representatives sought to obstruct it in any way they could. The Reichsrat was paralysed, first by the more traditional techniques of the filibuster (endless ranting and interminable debating) but also by outbreaks of rioting in the chamber which spilled out onto the streets. As a result, the Badeni government was brought down, the Czech language bill was withdrawn and, much more significantly, Franz Joseph was forced to use the rights established in article 14 of the 1867 constitution to rule by decree, with the help of the state bureaucracy. Nationalism had reduced parliament to a noisy irrelevance.

It is tempting to see this as proof that nationalism was a profoundly destructive force: something which would perhaps inevitably break up the Empire. But it must be remembered that neither the Germans nor the Czechs wanted to dismantle the Empire before 1914. Pessimists undoubtedly existed but so too did reformers, such as the heir to the throne Archduke Franz Ferdinand, who spoke of a new federal framework which might ease the tensions imposed by competing nationalisms.

c) Nationalism and the Introduction of Democracy

However, Franz Joseph knew that the Magyars would not accept a federal constitution. He had one other card to play. In 1907 the Emperor sanctioned what was perhaps the most imaginative act of his entire reign, the introduction of universal manhood suffrage in the western half of the Empire. Suddenly Cisleithania seemed to have transformed itself from a bureaucratic dictatorship into one of the most advanced states in Europe. Even the British ruling elite had not been rash enough to give all the working classes the vote. The aim behind this radical ploy appears to have been to bring the middle-class parties to heel. In general the nationalist parties, such as the Young Czechs, were supported by the middle classes. The working class by contrast tended to vote for the socialist Social Democratic Party. The Social Democratic Party was also a Marxist party pledged to the ending of the capitalist system. The Emperor hoped to use the spectre of Marxism to scare the wealthier middle-class parties into supporting the status quo. It could be also argued that, paradoxically, Marxism was perceived by the Monarchy as a kind of antidote to nationalism in that it actively urged people not to think of their identity in national terms but in class terms.

In some ways then the introduction of universal manhood suffrage was a brave shake of the political kaleidoscope in the hope that new and more acceptable patterns might emerge. Ironically, the result was to make the political system yet more unmanageable. The number of parties increased to such an extent that by 1911, the last pre-war election, over fifty parties competed for 516 seats. The proliferation of small parties meant that it was impossible to put together a loyal bloc of parties: there were simply too many small groups each with its own agenda, only too willing to bring a government down if its demands were not met. A young Adolf Hitler learnt his contempt for democracy whilst watching the Viennese parliament. In *Mein Kampf* he records it as

a wild gesticulating mass screaming all at once in every different key, presided by over by a good natured old uncle who was striving in the sweat of his brow to revive the dignity of the House by violently ringing his bell.

Similarly, an American journalist observing from the press gallery saw what he called

1 a band of madmen ... violently opening and shutting the lids of
  their desks. Others emitting a blaring sound from little toy
  trumpets; others strummed on Jew's harps; still others beat snare
  drums ... Every other faction had stored away a complete
5 assortment of such instruments of torture - whistles and sleigh
  bells, mouth harmonicas, cow bells and trombones ... merely for
  the business of making all legitimate business in the Reichsrat
  impossible.

Evidently the well-intentioned introduction of manhood suffrage had
created a kind of politcal insanity and the Reichsrat had been
transformed into an asylum. If Franz Joseph had hoped to use
democracy to counterbalance nationalism he found instead that the
problems were multiplied rather than solved. In effect, class allegiance
had been added to the existing issue of ethnic identity as another
powerful political force pulling people away from loyalty to the
Habsburgs. The Social Democrats controlled the working-class vote
and before long the Christian Socials emerged as the party of the lower
middle classes. A new type of popular politics was emerging: an age of
party machines, of propaganada and, above all, of loud charismatic
politicians. The prototype of the latter was Karl Leuger, the Christian
Social leader, who rallied the masses with simplistic slogans and attacks
on the Jews. (Adolf Hitler was deeply impressed by Leuger.) The
Emperor had, in effect, plunged the Empire into the age of mass politics:
a type of politics for which such a traditional and rather dull old man was
profoundly unsuited. It was no surprise then that in March 1914 the
Emperor prorogued his unworkable parliament, thus giving the peoples
of the Cisleithania no say in the subsequent July crisis which dragged
them into war. Curiously though, Franz Joseph's decision to go to war in
July 1914 was, in the short term, his most widely supported and popular
decision for years.

d) Nationalism in Hungary

Before discussing the extent of nationalism in the Transleithanian half of
the Empire it is very important to be clear about what is meant by
nationalism in this context. Basically there are two categories of
nationalism in question. Firstly there is the problem of what might be
called 'Yugoslav' nationalism. Here the question is, to what extent,
before 1914, was there a united movement of south Slavs in Hungary,
calling for an independent Yugoslavia? Secondly, there is the slightly
different question of how strong and/or significant was national feeling
amongst the separate national groups in Transleithania?
   It makes sense to take the first problem first. The *Ausgleich* left the

Magyars clearly in charge of their half of the Empire, and so complete was Magyar control that it has become customary to see the Magyars as a repressive ruling class, attempting to keep the lid firmly on south Slav nationalist ambitions. In this respect it is common to blame the so-called Magyarisation policy for the emergence of an increasingly militant south Slav movement which culminated in the creation of Yugoslavia after the war. Indeed, it is tempting to regard the assassination of Franz Ferdinand by a Bosnian Serb in 1914 as a direct result of Magyar oppressiveness. Thus it might be thought that the harsh policies of the Magyars are ultimately to blame for the Great War and indeed for the dissolution of the Empire. But is this true? To begin with it is important to scotch the notion that the Serbs in Bosnia-Herzegovina suffered under the harsh rule of the Magyars. Bosnia-Herzegovina was not part of the greater Kingdom of Hungary. After its annexation in 1908 it enjoyed an anomalous position within the Empire, in neither half of the Empire and yet jointly administered by both. In practice it was the Austrians and not the Hungarians who governed in Bosnia. Thus, the Magyars cannot be blamed for having driven the Bosnian Serbs into the Serbian nationalist camp.

Some assumptions may be easily dispelled but others are harder to challenge. It is undoubtedly perfectly logical to assume that there must have been some sort of 'Yugoslav' feeling in the Hungarian lands, given the eventual creation of Yugoslavia in 1919 out of large chunks of formerly Hungarian territory. But the evidence suggests that before the war the south Slavs did not form a united nationalist Yugoslav movement. In fact the Croats, Slovenes and Bosnian Serbs were frequently antagonistic toward each other. Each ethnic group felt its own ethnic identity quite strongly and, paradoxically, it was this narrow nationalism which undermined any hopes of a broader Yugoslav nationalism. Furthermore, the Magyars were very skilled at playing on these petty nationalist jealousies. For example, no sooner had the Magyars agreed to the terms of the *Ausgleich* than they began work on a similar sort of deal with the Croats within the eastern half of the Empire. As a result, in 1868 the Croats agreed to a constitutional arrangement, the *Nagodba*, which, although it allowed Budapest to nominate the Croatian president, nevertheless allowed Croatia to maintain its own parliament through which it could govern the Croatian territories. The Croats therefore came to enjoy a sense of superiority over the other south Slav groups and became in a sense junior partners in the governing of Transleithania. Effectively, the *Nagodba* allowed the Magyars to divide and rule.

The geographical distribution of the various groups within the framework of the whole Empire also worked against the emergence of an organised Yugoslav nationalism. For example, the majority of Slovenes came under the jurisdiction of Vienna, whilst their neighbours the Croats, with whom they had much in common, fell inside the eastern half of the Empire. Religion was another source of division between the south Slavs. The Croats were Roman Catholics, the Serbs were Orthodox, in Bosnia there were many Moslems, and in amongst all these communities there were many Jews. Undoubtedly such sharp religious divisions placed a serious obstacle in the way of any sense of 'Yugoslav' unity.

Nevertheless there were some signs of co-operation between south Slav groups. In the Croatian parliament the Serbs frequently combined with the Croats against Magyar influence. In 1912 a south Slav party was formed which called for the creation of a south Slav state. However, this state was intended to exist within the Empire, after the Dualist constitution had been suitably amended. In short, they wanted to change from Dualism to what has been called Trialism, in which the south Slavs would join the Austrians and Magyars as equal partners in a three sided constitution. Although this was in some ways the beginnings of a Yugoslav movement, it was always very weak. The Serbs resented the way the Croats and the Slovenes sought to dominate the movement and, as a result, the movement was so internally divided that it had very little chance of political success. The fact seems to be that before 1914 there was no movement of any significance calling for an independent Yugoslavia. Only during the war, and then only after Franz Joseph had died and the war had taken a turn for the worse, did the notion of an independent Yugoslavia become popular.

What of the second sort of nationalism, the separate nationalisms of the individual ethnic groups in the Hungarian lands? In political terms nationalism posed very little threat to the dominance of the Magyars. There are many reasons for this but the prime one must be the electoral system itself. Hungarian electoral laws allowed only 6 per cent of the adult population to vote, thereby creating a situation in which, though the Magyars were less than half of the population of Transleithania, they obtained over 90 per cent of the seats in the Hungarian parliament. Thus it was extremely difficult for Slav groups, or indeed non-Slav groups such as the Romanians, to elect enough representatives to exert any influence in Budapest. For example, in the 1910 election non-Magyar candidates combined achieved only 8 seats out of 393 in the Hungarian parliament. Clearly, nationalism, which had reduced the Vienna parliament to a farce, was barely felt at all in the parliament in Budapest.

But such impotence need not be entirely attributed to the oppressive laws of the Magyars. Most of the peoples of the Hungarian lands were simply not interested in nationalist politics. The mass of the population were semi-literate peasants with more interest in pigs than politics. Such nationalists as there were tended to come from the educated middle classes and these were so few in number as to be politically negligible.

Overall, it does not seem that the Magyars needed to fight to hold the lid down on nationalism of any sort. Politically, the Magyars had achieved a tight grip on the governmental process, a position strengthened by their increasingly tight grip on the social and cultural life of the Hungarian Kingdom.

i) Magyarisation

In addition to all the above reasons for the weakness of opposition nationalist groups is the fact that they were subject to the policy of Magyarisation. This policy aimed at the forcible assimilation of Slavs, Germans and Jews into the dominant Magyar culture. The principal instrument for such ethnic engineering was the education system. In 1883 the Hungarian language became compulsory in all secondary schools. In 1891 the Kindergarten Act enforced the use of Hungarian at even the most junior level. Every town in the Hungarian half of the Empire was given an official Magyar name. The government even encouraged people to adopt Magyar names. So successful was this policy in central Hungary that the percentage of people describing themselves as Magyar for the census actually rose remarkably in the second half of the century. In Budapest, for example, the population changed from being 75 per cent German-speaking in 1848 to 80 per cent Hungarian by 1900. This phenomenon was repeated in all the major towns of central Hungary. Jews, in particular, opted for Magyar identities in their thousands. This may have been in part to escape anti-semitism but it was also because becoming Hungarian was a passport to economic and social advancement: the state, the civil service, the judiciary, and the professional and business worlds were all but closed to non-Magyars. Anyone with ambition felt the pressure to adopt the Hungarian tongue and for that reason Magyarisation successfully increased the numbers of official Hungarians in the Kingdom.

However, it should be added that the peasant peoples of the peripheral regions of the Hungarian Kingdom, most of them Slavs, were largely immune to such pressures by virtue of their profoundly unsophisticated lifestyles. The Slovakian or Romanian peasant farmer had little or no use for the Hungarian language. He or she did not hope to enter government or the civil service. The uncomplicated culture of these people made them resistant to most forms of change. For the ruling class this was a mixed blessing: the common people could not be forcibly Magyarised but nor could they be easily interested in the abstract ideas of the nationalists.

ii) Magyar Separatism

Oddly, it was Hungarian nationalism that most threatened the *Ausgleich*. Immediately after the settlement Louis Kossuth, the hero of 1848, wrote from exile denouncing the Compromise as a sell-out to the Habsburgs. Initially his opinions were unpopular but towards the end of the century, as Hungary appeared to be less economically dependent upon Austria, the movement for independence grew in momentum. In 1894 Kossuth returned to Hungary as a corpse. But a dead man can sometimes be more effective than a live one. As a dead man he entered the realms of myth and legend. He was given a ceremonial funeral. There followed a wave of nostalgic patriotism that enabled his son, Francis to lead the so-called Independence Party to significant success at the polls. By the turn of the century the Independence Party was the main opposition to the pro-*Ausgleich* Liberal Party led by Stephan Tisza. The Liberals had dominated politics since 1867, being the party most dedicated to Magyar supremacy. But by the turn of the century their grip was beginning to weaken. The fact that both parties - the governing Liberals and the opposing Independents - were dominated by Magyars highlights both the divisions which were beginning to open up within the Magyar ruling class and the relative insignificance of non-Magyar parties.

There were numerous issues over which the separatist nationalists could rock the Dualist boat. There was constant friction over the so-called tax quota - the amount which Hungary would contribute to central funds. But it was the question of the army which was to precipitate the nearest thing to a constitutional crisis before 1914. In 1903 a bill was discussed in the Hungarian parliament which called for an increase in the number of Hungarians in the Imperial army. This was the opportunity the nationalists had long sought. They demanded that a separate Hungarian army be set up, within which Hungarian would be the language of command. In addition, they insisted that the army would fly the Hungarian, rather than the Imperial, flag. Franz Joseph refused to accept such proposals. In turn the Hungarian parliament refused to grant him his reform of the army. The constitution and indeed the *Ausgleich* was in crisis. An election was called. The Liberals, seeing no way out of the impasse, deliberately chose to lose the election. As a result, in 1905 the Independence Party suddenly found itself in power and the Dualist system began to look very fragile indeed. At first Franz Joseph resolved his problems using brute force. Using the emergency powers granted him in the constitution, he resorted to ruling Hungary by decree. But this was clearly no solution as it tended to fuel the flames of separatist nationalism. The eventual solution was rather more subtle. The Emperor threatened to introduce universal manhood suffrage in Hungary. At a stroke he brought the nationalists to heel as the proposed change would have empowered the resentful south Slav peoples. It might even have facilitated the rise of the Social Democrat Party which was pledged to create a socialist Hungary in which the workers rather than the landed classes would dominate. In short, Franz Joseph was threatening to put an end to Magyar hegemony. Overnight the nationalists became reasonable and the political log-jam was broken. Franz Joseph duly withdrew his bill for franchise reform. The army bill went through. The Independence Party rapidly lost credibility and by 1910 the Liberals were back in power (renamed for no apparent reason as The Party of Work) where they stayed until the dissolution of the Empire. For the Emperor it was an ambiguous triumph. He had achieved the desired changes in the organisation of the army but it was also apparent that he had allowed the Magyars to establish the principle that there would be no move towards democracy in Transleithania at a time when the rest of Europe seemed to be moving almost inexorably towards greater popular participation in politics. Franz Joseph even introduced universal manhood suffrage in Cisleithania in 1907. Arguably, if Europe's future was democratic, the Magyars were chaining the Habsburgs to the past.

2 Habsburg Foreign Policy, 1867-1914

a) Accepting Defeat in the West

The defeat at Sadowa was a severe blow to Habsburg prestige which left the Empire very uncertain of its future role in the European balance of power. The Emperor undoubtedly entertained notions of striking back at Prussia and reversing the verdict of 1866. His foreign minister, Beust, was urged to look for ways to reassert Austria's primacy in Germany. But Franz Joseph was not being realistic. Beust analysed the situation more shrewdly. His policies were aimed not so much at defeating Bismarck but at preventing Prussia from expanding any further. To this end he sought to strengthen links with the southern states of Germany that were, as yet, not part of the enlarged Prussian state known as the North German Confederation. Beust was aware that Bismarck had ambitions to swallow up the southern states in a unified Reich and he hoped to prevent this from occurring. It was, then, as a counterweight to Prussia that Beust felt that Austria could retain some power and influence in German affairs.

The key figure in Habsburg calculations was the rather unpredictable French Emperor, Napoleon III. The French were also alarmed at the rapid growth of Prussian power. Napoleon III shared with Franz Joseph the conviction that Prussia should not be allowed to expand any more and that, if possible, she should be taught a lesson. Their shared anti-Prussianism led the two Emperors into a number of secret meetings in the later 1860s. However, Franz Joseph was advised by Andrássy, the most powerful politician in Hungary, that Hungarians would not support a war against Prussia. The *Ausgleich*, which had been given partly to win Hungarian support for a war against Prussia, proved to be precisely the reason why no such war was feasible. Andrássy insisted that the Dual Monarchy should adopt a position of 'armed neutrality' on the question of Franco-Prussian relations. Nevertheless, it was clear that Habsburg sympathies lay with France.

But Napoleon III miscalculated badly. In 1870 Bismarck provoked Napoleon into declaring war against Prussia. Once again the Prussian army moved so swiftly and so effectively that victory was quickly won. Prussia had not only defeated the French but also absorbed the southern German states into a unified Reich. Before the war Franz Joseph hoped that Prussia might be decisively weakened by war with France. Instead the Franco-Prussian War of 1870-1 proved to be another violent growth spurt in the creation of the new German superpower. Inevitably after 1871 the Habsburgs began to shift their gaze away from Germany towards their eastern borders, and in particular to the Balkans for a new sphere of influence. This switch of priorities from west to east dramatically changed the nature of the problems which now headed the agenda for the foreign ministers who followed Beust after his departure in 1871.

b) Austro-Russian Relations: (I) The Balkan Question, 1871-96

Although the details of Habsburg foreign policy in the Near East after 1871 can seem amazingly detailed and obscure, the fundamental problem was relatively straightforward. To put it at its simplest, throughout the nineteenth century the peoples of the Balkans had been ruled over by the Ottoman Empire but, by the last quarter of the century, Turkish authority was rapidly breaking down. The decline of this so-called 'sick man of Europe' created a power vacuum in the Balkans into which the Austro-Hungarian and Russian empires were only too willing to rush. In a sense then, Habsburg foreign policy between the years 1871 and 1914 can be seen as one long story of Austro-Russian tension, culminating in a terrible war.

However, the issue is complicated by the fact that the peoples of the Balkans were discovering their own nationalist ambitions and were not necessarily happy to be absorbed by either Russia or Austria-Hungary. Serbia, in particular, after having gained her formal independence from the Ottoman Empire in 1878, after 60 years of being independent in all but name, became the focus of south Slav nationalism. This was an ominous development for the Habsburgs given the large numbers of Serbs and other south Slav groups within their borders. In addition, the Russians had traditionally acted as the protectors of the southern Slavs in the Balkans, being the self-styled leaders of the so-called Panslav movement. In Vienna Russia was perceived as simply using Panslavism as a mask behind which to extend her own influence in the area.

After the fall of Beust in 1871, Franz Joseph appointed Andrássy as his foreign minister. Andrássy was strongly anti-Russian in outlook and could be relied upon to stand up to Russian expansionism and intrigue in the Balkans. However, he was not in favour of further Austro-Hungarian expansion in the region. He reasoned that this would involve swallowing up yet more Slavs which would, in turn, tilt the ethnic balance in the Hungarian half of the Monarchy dangerously against his own class, the ruling Magyar nobility. Franz Joseph accepted Andrássy's argument that the Empire should neither expand nor contract but should, instead, dedicate itself to preserving the delicate balance of power in the Balkans for as long as possible. To this end Andrássy devoted all his immense diplomatic skills. He was aware that the Empire was probably too weak to risk a war with Russia and therefore sought allies against the perceived Russian menace. Of the other Great Powers only Germany (as Prussia had become in 1871) could or would offer Andrássy the kind of assurances he sought. Bismarck was enthusiastic to find a way of healing old wounds if only to reduce the chances of an Austro-French alliance against Germany. By 1872 Andrássy and Bismarck had not only become friends but they had also persuaded their respective heads of state to visit each other. In effect, an unofficial alliance had come into being.

But Andrássy's achievement was in some ways an illusion. In reality he had become the prisoner of Bismarck's designs, and the German chancellor had a rather different agenda to that of the Habsburg foreign minister. Bismarck's underlying aim was to make sure that France remained isolated. To that end it was also important for Germany to seek an alliance with Russia in order to preclude any possibility of the Franco-Russian alliance of Bismarck's nightmares. Thus, much too Andrássy's astonishment and horror, in 1873 he found himself dragged by his new German ally into a three sided alliance of Germany, Russia and Austria-Hungary known as the 'League of the Three Emperors' (*Dreikaiserbund*). The substance of this fine-sounding arrangement, from the Habsburg point of view, was the Convention of Schönbrunn, by which Austria-Hungary and Russia agreed to consult each other before taking action on any foreign policy issue in which there might be a conflict of interest.

Andrássy was not entirely happy with the benefits of membership of the *Dreikaiserbund*. The Convention of Schönbrunn may have brought some sense of security, but the whole agreement also established a distinctly unwanted bond between Germany and Russia. Nevertheless some progress had apparently been made: Germany had been transformed from an old enemy into a friend and Russia had agreed to talk rather than fight. In addition, in some ways the *Dreikaiserbund* had restored the status of the Empire. Once again she seemed a great power on a par with the now mighty Germany and imperial Russia. But in 1875 a crisis began to unfold in the Balkans which tested the League to its limits. The crisis was initially ignited by an uprising in Bosnia-Herzegovina against Turkish rule. Although the Turks were at first quite successful in suppressing this rebellion, the flames of nationalist aspiration spread rapidly into neighbouring areas. In 1876 Serbia and Montenegro joined in the war against the Ottoman authorities. Confronted with the prospect of a seemingly imminent collapse of Ottoman authority in the Balkans, the Austrians and the Russians, acting in the spirit of the Schönbrunn Convention, met to discuss their joint response to he crisis. In the summer of 1876 they concluded the so-called Reichstadt Agreements in which they decided that should Turkey be defeated they would carve up its territories between themselves, with Austria-Hungary acquiring most of Bosnia-Herzegovina and Russia gaining southern Bessarabia. Serbia, Montenegro, Bulgaria and Roumelia would be allowed to emerge as smallish independent states.

However, Andrássy was a reluctant signatory to the Reichstadt agreements and he was relieved when the armies of the Ottoman Empire defeated the Serbian-led coalition in 1876, thereby apparently removing any need for Austrian or Russian intervention. But the crisis was not yet over. The Tsar was unhappy with the way the Turks treated the defeated peoples of Bosnia-Herzegovina and demanded that the Turks grant the peoples of this area some limited rights of self-government. The row over this issue brought Russia into the war against the Turks. But the Tsar had been careful to obtain Austrian neutrality before declaring war on Turkey. In January 1877 Austria and Russia had agreed in the Budapest Convention that Austrian would acquire the right to occupy a self-governing Bosnia-Herzegovina should the Russians beat the Turks, as they were highly likely to do. The Russians for their part agreed that they would limit their expansion to the more easterly parts of the Balkans.

But the Russians also knew that the Habsburg armies were not strong enough to push Russia out of the Balkans once established. In the event, Russian armies moved rapidly against the Turks and enjoyed such success that the Tsar was persuaded by the Panslavists at home that he should seize this opportunity to settle the Balkan question firmly in Russia's favour. In March 1878 the Tsar forced the Turks to sign a settlement, the Treaty of San Stefano, which not only conspicuously failed to deliver Bosnia and Herzegovina to the Austrians, as promised at Budapest, but also created a 'big Bulgaria' which would have become a Russian client state.

Andrássy was outraged at what he regarded, with some justification, as a betrayal. He turned to Bismarck in the hope that he might back him in a war against Russia. Bismarck was not prepared to go to war for an issue which could bring no territorial gain for Germany. His celebrated remark that 'the Balkans are not worth the bones of a single Pomeranian grenadier' captures the spirit of detached contempt with which the German chancellor viewed the problem. But he was anxious that the now ruptured *Dreikaiserbund* should be put back together again. For this reason he, along with the British prime minister Disraeli, following traditional British Russophobic foreign policy, moved swiftly to set up a Congress of Great Powers to resolve the tensions caused by the Russian actions.

At the subsequent Congress of Berlin in June 1878 Bismarck, posing as an 'honest broker', with the support of Disraeli, persuaded the Russians to back down. The Treaty of San Stefano was effectively torn up. The Russians relinquished the idea of a large Bulgarian client state, accepting the creation a far smaller independent Bulgaria. Austria-Hungary gained the right to occupy Bosnia-Herzegovina, although it was to remain under Turkish sovereignty. In addition to this, the Monarchy obtained the right to station garrisons in the strategically important Sanjak of Novi-Bazar, although it also remained technically under Turkish rule.

In some ways the Congress of Berlin brought a temporary stability to the region and might be seen as a success for Andrássy's anti-Russian policies. But, perversely, Andrássy's triumph was perceived by many in the Empire as a disaster. Indeed, it seems that Andrássy had managed to offend almost all important sections of opinion in the Monarchy. The Germans and Magyars regarded the partial acquisition of Bosnia-Herzegovina as an unwanted burden of extra unruly Slavs to govern which could only destabilise the precarious ethnic balance and exacerbate the problems posed by Slav nationalism. At a more pragmatic level, it was argued, correctly, that the cost of involvement in these provinces would be greater than any possible financial gain. The more aggressive or 'forward party' in Vienna which had actually wanted a war with Russia felt that Bismarck had sold them short. Franz Joseph, though normally pacific, also seems to have shared some of their frustrations with the Monarchy's lack of clear-cut territorial acquisitions. These various and contradictory criticisms swelled about Andrássy making his political position increasingly untenable. Ironically Andrássy was only too aware of the weaknesses and flaws in the Berlin settlement but justified his actions on the grounds that the Emperor had been against war. But this eminently sensible defence did not appease his critics and he was forced from office in 1879.

But Andrássy left one very important legacy. Just before stepping down he was able to secure the conclusion of a formal alliance with Bismarckian Germany, which secured the promise of German military assistance for the Habsburgs in the event of an attack by Russia upon them. This so-called Dual Alliance was destined to hold good for almost 40 years. It was in many ways intended to deter Russia from war. It was therefore in some sense a peace initiative. Both Bismarck and Andrássy saw the Dual Alliance in those terms. The fact that it was these two powers who encouraged each other to risk a great war in 1914 is surely a testament not to the folly of Andrássy's or Bismarck's thinking but to the recklessness of the men who inherited their diplomatic system.

The threat from Russia seemed to decline a little in 1881 when Bismarck managed to resurrect the Three Emperors' League under the modified title of the Three Emperors' Alliance. The terms of this alliance bound the signatories to a neutral postion in the event of any of the three powers becoming involved in a war with another country.

However, the Alliance was essentially destroyed in 1886 when Austria-Hungary chose to back Bulgaria in its efforts to shake itself free of Russian domination. After 1886 Bismarck was not able to revive his dream of a grand alliance of the conservative powers of Europe, although this was in large part due to the fact that the new Kaiser in Germany, William II, forced him to resign in 1890 thereby perhaps not only removing Europe's most skilful politician but also its best guarantee of peace.

But Austria-Hungary had little immediate reason to worry. In 1882 Italy had transformed the Dual into the Triple Alliance, and in 1887 the Empire had signed the Mediterranean Agreements with Britain which were designed to present a united naval front against Russian expansion in the Mediterranean or Black Seas. In addition, some of the key Balkan states - Romania, Serbia and Bulgaria - all appeared pro-Habsburg if only by virtue of their growing resentment of Russian interference in their affairs. In short, as the end of century loomed Austria-Hungary must have felt very secure against the Russian menace both on land and at sea.

c) Austro-Russian Relations: (II) Co-operation and Agreement, 1897-1908

At the turn of the century relations between Austria-Hungary and Russia improved and the Balkans appeared for a while to be no longer a source of friction. The reasons for this *rapprochement* were quite varied. Both empires had internal political problems, and Russia was increasingly absorbed with the threat posed by Japan to her terrritories in the far east. Mainly for these reasons both sides actively sought to defuse the Balkan time-bomb.

In 1897 Austria-Hungary negotiated an entente in which both sides agreed not to seek expansion in the Balkans. This agreement lasted for about ten years and effectively enabled both empires to focus their attentions elsewhere for the next decade. The agreement proved to be surprisingly durable when put to the test. In 1903 a rebellion by the Macedonians led to joint intervention by the two empires and the signing of the so-called Mürzsteg Programme which reasserted the territorial status quo and provided armed forces to put teeth into the agreement. The Mürzsteg Programme is proof that Balkan national-ism in itself did not necessarily have to drag Austria-Hungary and Russia into war. For a brief period, now largely overlooked by historians, the Balkans actually served to bring the Habsburgs and the Romanovs closer together. So convincing was this new-found co-operation that Aehrenthal, the Habsburg foreign minister, sugges-ted that the *Dreikaiserbund* be resurrected.

But events conspired slowly to erode the basis of the new-found harmony. In 1903 a new and more aggressive dynasty in Serbia stoked the flames of Balkan nationalism. In 1905 Russia lost her war with Japan in the far east and swung her attentions rapidly back to the Balkan theatre. In 1907 Russia joined France and Britain in the Triple Entente, leaving Europe clearly and ominously divided into two blocs. More seriously, in 1908 the so-called Young Turks seized power in the Turkish Empire. This was an event which created a great deal of uncertainty. Would the Turkish Empire emerge stronger or weaker? Either eventuality seemed likely to upset the fragile conditions of shared Austro-Turkish rule in Bosnia-Herzegovina. It was Habsburg efforts to find a solution to this crisis which precipitated the breakdown of the Austro-Russian entente and arguably set the two empires on course for a fatal collision.

d) Austro-Russian Relations: (III) The Road to Ruin, 1908-14

Initially the Young Turk revolution brought Austria-Hungary and Russia closer together. Aehrenthal and Izvolski, the Russian foreign minister, met to consider a joint response. No record of their negotiations remains but it seems that Izvolski agreed in principle to allow Austria-Hungary to annex Bosnia-Herzegovina in return for Austrian support for Russia's ambitions to achieve free passage through the Dardanelles Strait. But such careful diplomatic groundwork was suddenly destroyed in October 1908 when the Imperial armies invaded Bosnia-Herzegovina without giving the Tsar any prior warning. Even Izvolski was taken by surprise. Crucially Izvolski had not had time to sell his bargain to the Tsar and his ministers and the Russian court therefore denounced the Habsburg invasion as naked expansionism. To complicate matters Serbia also protested, claiming that the rights of the Slav peoples had been infringed. This in turn allowed the Tsar to play out his chosen Panslavist role as protector of the Slavs.

Behind the din of Panslavist rhetoric both Russia and Serbia had hidden agendas. Serbia objected to Habsburg imperialism because it obstructed their own. They had wanted to acquire Bosnia-Herzegovina in order to construct a Greater Serbia. Russia looked favourably on Serbian expansionism because it would give them a powerful client-state in the Balkans. Oddly or perhaps typically, no one seems to have given any thought to the wishes of the peoples of Bosnia-Herzegovina.

Bosnia-Herzegovina was a distinctly multi-ethnic province, a patchwork of Serbs, Croats and Muslims. The Bosnian Serbs, about 40 per cent of the population, hankered for unity with Serbia but the other groups were far less enthusiastic. In the final analysis the views of the Muslim or Croat factions of Bosnia-Herzegovina were irrelevant: they had no army or powerful ally to stand up for them. In the event the pawn was taken by Austria-Hungary. To add insult to injury the Russians were eventually forced to recognise this by the heavy-handed intervention of

Kaiser William of Germany who informed the Tsar that Germany would stand by its ally in the event of any hostilities. Russia was in no position to call the Kaiser's bluff, having not fully recovered from the military defeat at the hands of the Japanese in 1905. Serbia too was forced to accept the *fait accompli* by the use of threats, emanating this time from Vienna.

The consequences of the Bosnian crisis were profound. Most obviously, the Austro-Russian entente was shattered. In its place arose a lingering resentment in Russia and a determination, backed by an expanding army, never to let such a humiliation happen again. Panslavist feeling in Russia was given a great boost: the link between Belgrade (the capital of Serbia) and St. Petersburg was considerably strengthened. In addition to this, the apparent bully-boy tactics of Austria and Germany also served to push Britain and France closer to Russia. As a result, Europe appeared to be increasingly divided into two hostile alliance systems. In short, the crisis of 1908 ensured that any subsequent crisis in the Balkans would endanger the peace of all of Europe.

In 1912 Aehrenthal died and was replaced by Count Berchtold, but the policies remained much the same. Berchtold also identified Serbian expansionism as the principal menace in the Balkans, not least because it would in some respects be tantamount to Russian expansion. But it was also feared because it was thought that Russo-Serbian successes would stimulate the nationalist demands of the Bosnian Serbs within the Empire. To many observers in Vienna the growth of Slav nationalism in the south of the Empire seemed to threaten the total disintegration of the Empire into national fragments. For this reason the Serbian question was regarded as the most serious issue on Berchtold's agenda and the aim of his immediate policy was containment.

However, Serbia was determined to expand. In particular it was determined to exploit the decline of the Turkish Empire in order to create the dreamed-of Greater Serbia. In the Autumn of 1912 Serbia, Bulgaria, Greece and Montenegro combined to form a Balkan League against the Turks, and to launch what has become known as the First Balkan War. The result was a crushing defeat for the Turks and their almost complete expulsion from Europe. The Balkan states shared out the spoils amongst themselves. Berchtold recognised that there was little that the Monarchy could do to reverse events, but nevertheless he sought to appeal to the other great powers as a way of curbing Serbian success. In this policy he was partially successful. In particular, he did not want to see the formerly land-locked Serbia expand onto the Adriatic coastline. Britain, France and Germany were also sympathetic to this because they too did not want to see a pro-Russian state acquire a port in the Mediterranean. Thus was born the London Conference of Great Powers which in 1913 met to examine this problem. The solution was Albania. An Albanian state was created along the eastern Adriatic coastline not so much out of respect for the rights of Albanian people to self-determination but out of the immediate need to put an obstacle in the Serbian path. The Serbs had little choice but to accept this.

But Serbia's frustrated energies rapidly rebounded into the Balkan interior. In 1913 the Balkan states began squabbling amongst themselves over the spoils of the First Balkan War. The squabbles led swiftly to the so-called Second Balkan war. This time Serbia and Greece lined up against Bulgaria. Unsurprisingly, Berchtold sought to back Bulgaria but his hopes were frustrated by the intervention of Romania on the Serbian side. The Second Balkan War was therefore not only another victory for Serbia, but it was also a defeat for Berchtold's policy of containment.

The rapid expansion of Serbia created a climate of near hysteria in military circles in Vienna. Military leaders, and indeed politicians, were agreed that a clash with Serbia was inevitable. Serbia, for its part, was undeniably encouraging the Bosnian Serbs to undertake a nationalist uprising against the Monarchy. But, although many of the Bosnian Serbs did want to be 'liberated' by Serbia, neither they nor the Serbian forces could achieve it alone. For the Serbs to be successful the Habsburgs would have to be provoked into taking the offensive because only in that way could Serbia hope to obtain Russian defensive backing.

Emperor Franz Joseph was extremely reluctant to take military action against Serbia. The Emperor remembered only too painfully how wars launched in 1859 and 1866 had led to the loss of territory. Another war might well lead to total disintegration. But many of the leading political and military figures around him in 1913-14 seemed paralysed by a curious pessimistic fatalism. Indeed, it was the mood of despair that prompted many to call for action that would at least settle the question once and for all.

In the end it fell to a young Bosnian Serb called Gavrilo Princip to put the Monarchy out of its misery. On 28 June 1914 the heir to the Habsburg throne, Archduke Franz Ferdinand, paid an official state visit to Sarajevo, the capital of Bosnia-Herzegovina, in order to popularise the Monarchy in its new province. A Serbian terrorist group, known as 'The Black Hand', decided to attempt an assassination of the heir in the hope that this would spark the long-awaited war. The event itself was a sinister farce. Gavrilo Princip bungled his first attempt to kill the Archduke. But then fate took a hand. The Archduke's chauffeur took a wrong turning and in effect delivered the victim and his wife to the incompetent assassin for a second effort. Franz Ferdinand and his wife were shot dead from point blank range and the Great Powers began their slow diplomatic dance into war.

e) From Assassination to War

The first step was the Habsburg assumption that the Serbian

government had some prior knowledge of the assassination plot and had therefore to be taught a lesson. Historians seem to agree that the Serbian government, whilst not actually directly involved with the Black Hand, did know of its methods and were indirectly providing funds for it. It was decided in Vienna, with nervous and somewhat reluctant support from the Hungarian prime minister Tisza, to send the Serbs an ultimatum so stiffly worded that they could not possibly meet its terms. The ultimatum was designed to become a pretext for war. However, Berchtold and Franz Joseph were by no means insensitive to the wider European alliance system. To put it bluntly, the politicians in Vienna had to weigh up very carefully the chances of Russia coming to Serbia's aid. For this reason Berchtold's first action was to consult with the Kaiser. On 5 July 1914 the Kaiser gave the Emperor what has become known as 'the Blank Cheque': an assurance that Germany would come to the Monarchy's aid no matter what she chose to do. Some historians have seen this as a reckless incitement to war, others have stressed the Kaiser's belief that German assurances would serve, as they had in 1908, to persuade Russia to back down, thereby allowing Austria-Hungary her short punitive war against Serbia. But events took a different course. Armed with the Blank Cheque, Austria-Hungary delivered her extremely provocative ultimatum to the Serbs on 23 July. Berchtold later recalled in his memoirs the extent to which the Emperor was aware of the significance of this moment:

1 The Emperor was fully conscious of the serious, I would even say tragic, nature of this historic moment ... However difficult it may have been for him to take a decision which he must have known would have severe consequences, he took it with dignity and
5 serenity, and gave, without hesitation, the order for it to be carried out.

The Serbs met all the terms of the ultimatum but one: they refused to relinquish control of their armed forces whilst the Habsburg forces entered the country to carry out an investigation. Thus on 28 July 1914 the Habsburgs declared war on Serbia. The Emperor remained fatalistic announcing that,

1 It was my most profound wish to devote the years which God in his mercy may still grant me to working for peace and to protecting my peoples from the heavy burdens and sacrifices of war. But the fates have seen otherwise. The machinations of a hostile Power, moved
5 by hatred, compel me after many long years of peace to take up the sword to preserve the honour of my Monarchy.

On the same day Russia began a partial mobilisation of her armies. On 31 July she ordered complete mobilisation. On 1 August, after an ultimatum had expired the previous day, Germany declared war on Russia. At this juncture German military plans came into operation. The German 'Schlieffen Plan' was based on the plausible premise that Germany could not fight a war in the east without exposing herself to invasion from France in the west. Thus the Schlieffen Plan involved a rapid strike into France, in order to prevent the possibility of having to fight a war on two fronts. On 4 August Germany invaded Belgium on route for France. On the same day Britain entered the war against Germany, ostensibly to defend Belgium. Oddly Britain and France did not bother to announce a formal declaration of war against the Austro-Hungarian Empire until 12 August, but such niceties did not matter much since the Monarchy's fate was now irrevocably tied to Germany's. It was a link that was destined to destroy the Habsburg Empire.

3) Conclusion: War and Dissolution

a) The Impact of War

At first war was wonderful. It brought a temporary unity to the Empire. National aspirations were forgotten, social divisions were overlooked and young men were thrilled to enlist to fight for the most ancient of family names. In the late summer of 1914 few people could have guessed that the Habsburg Monarchy was about to enter upon the final act of its long history.

However, the course of the war soon brought disillusionment. The initial purpose of the war had been simply to crush Serbia but the threat from the Russian armies in Galicia effectively opened up a second front and it rapidly became apparent that the Imperial army was not prepared either strategically or in terms of resources to cope with this development. By the end of 1914 the Imperial army had suffered serious reverses against the Russians and had been thrown out of Serbia. The cost in terms of men was extremely high. In the first six months of the war three-quarters of a million men were lost. There were of course some victories; notably against the Russians in 1915 and against the Italians at Caporetto in 1917, but overall the Imperial army proved to be a rather inefficient military machine.

There are a number of reasons why the army performed badly. At the simplest level the military planning was inadequate and grave miscalculations were made. But there were more profound problems which in some ways grew out of the very structure of the Empire itself. The most often cited weakness within the army was the divisions amongst the nationalities; a weakness that clearly mirrored the nature of the state. As the war went on these divisions became an increasingly important source of difficulties. For example, the deaths of so many German officers in the first two years of the war led inevitably to the creation of officers from the Slav groups. This created resentments and at a more practical level often created language problems. More importantly, many of these nationalities were susceptible to nationalist propaganda, some of which actually advocated surrender on the grounds that the allies were supporting the aspirations of the Slav peoples for independence. Inevitably this must have been a large factor in the increasingly high desertion rate that plagued the Imperial army in the last phase of the war.

At the political level other problems inherent in the nature of the Dual Monarchy undermined the war effort. Not the least of these was the death of Franz Joseph at the age of 86 in November 1916. The old man had held the Empire together since 1848: while he lived there was stability. But the succession was always likely to create problems. His own son, Crown Prince Rudolph, had killed himself in 1889 and the next in line, Franz Ferdinand had been assassinated in 1914. According to the principle of hereditary succession, Franz Joseph's successor was his great nephew, Karl. But Karl was not well-suited to his task. He was described by a contemporary as a 30-year-old man 'with the appearance of a 20-year-old youth, who thinks, speaks and acts like a 10-year-old boy'. This may be too harsh but it is certain that Karl was rather an indecisive Emperor, with liberal convictions but without the personal courage to act on them.

The economic structure of the Empire was also exposed as unable to sustain a prolonged military campaign. Most fundamentally of all, in the last two years of the war food shortages began to create crises in the major cities and even within the armed forces. The western half of the Monarchy, which had been dependent for grain on the east, found itself severely short of supplies. Galicia a rich source of grain in pre-war years had become a battlefield. Those who had grain in Hungary tended to want to give it to Hungarians rather than Austrians. The myth of the unity in duality was gradually and cruelly exposed.

The war put the Empire to the test and found it wanting. Only peace could have saved it from disintegration. But the military and political leaders were not prepared to seek peace. They were not prepared to act independently of Germany and the German High Command was determined to press for outright victory. In a very real sense Austria-Hungary had become so dependent upon Germany that it had lost the will to govern itself. The decisions that would determine its future were taken in Berlin rather than Vienna.

b) Dissolution

At the end of the war the Austro-Hungarian Empire was broken up. Out of the Imperial rubble emerged the new states of Czechoslovakia and Yugoslavia, along with a reinvented Poland. The Habsburg Empire, for 400 years the largest power in central Europe, was consigned to the rubbish heap of history. But why was the price of defeat so high? Why was the Empire dismantled while Germany, her arguably more aggressive ally, was allowed to survive largely intact?

In some ways the answer lies with the allies. It is a fact that neither Britain nor France saw the break up of the Empire as part of their initial war aims. Instead in 1914 they saw the existence of the Habsburg Empire as preferable to either Russian expansion or an anarchy of central European nationalisms. But, unfortunately for the Habsburgs, these principles changed as the war progressed. By 1918 such considerations seemed less important than simple victory in a war which had gone on longer and been more appalling than anyone predicted. As a result, the allies began to see the nationalist aspirations of the peoples of the Empire as a weakness to be exploited.

The turning point occurred in January 1918 when the American president, Woodrow Wilson, issued his 14 points declaring that the rights of nations to self-determination would be the guiding principle behind any peace settlement. Suddenly defeat appeared to Slav nationalists within the Empire as a potential liberation from German or Magyar rule. Wilson's declared aim of establishing a new Poland even undermined the loyalty of the Habsburg's most reliable Slav group. Wilson's 'self-determination' proved to be the allies' most potent weapon against the Austro-Hungarian Empire.

But this threat was exacerbated by the Monarchy itself. There can be no doubt that in the last two years of the war there was a radicalisation of the nationality question. Not only Czechs but almost all the Slav groups became more militant and demanded some sort of concessions as the price for their continued loyalty. But the most astonishing aspect of this development is surely the response of the Empire. The political leaders in Vienna and Budapest did nothing. Only when it was too late, in October 1918 when the Empire had all but disintegrated, did the timid Emperor offer up a proposal for a new federal constitution. It was a dead letter even before the Magyars, with typical and stupid obstinacy, refused to accept it. Evidently any attempt to square the nationalist circle would have required a politician with the diplomatic skills of a Metternich. No such man was available. But, although the dissolution of the Empire was caused, in part, by the radicalisation of Slav nationalism in the last year of the war, more important than the nationalist agitations or indeed Magyar bloody-mindedness or the sufferings caused by war, was surely the fatal lack of political initiative displayed in the face of these urgent problems.

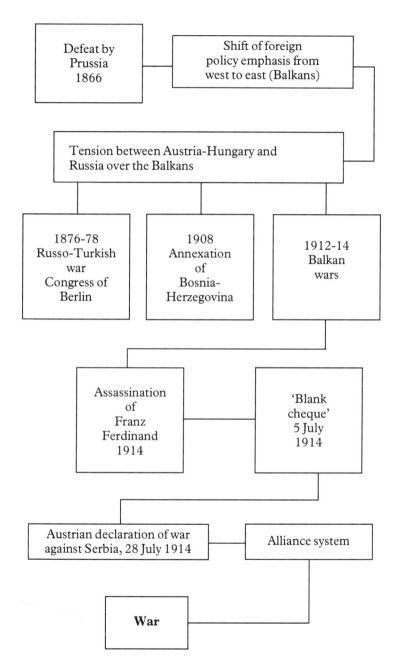

Summary - The Habsburg Empire, 1867-1914

Making notes on 'The Habsburg Empire, 1867-1914'

Clearly this chapter covers a long period of time and there is a great deal of information to learn. The simplest way to deal with the problem of learning such a vast amount of detail is probably to draw up a chronology of key dates. However, although this is helpful as a necessary 'background' exercise, examiners are not that interested in your ability to remember lists of dates. Therefore you should attempt when taking notes to relate what you are writing to key issues or ideas. A good way to do this will be to compile your notes by answering the following questions.

1   Why was the rise of nationalism a great threat to the Habsburg Empire?
2   What were the aims of the Czech nationalists?
2.1 Did these aims threaten the existence of the Empire?
3   Why did Franz Joseph introduce universal suffrage in Cisleithania?
3.1 What were the results of this action?
4   What is the meaning of the term 'Magyarisation'?
4.1 In what way did the Magyars block the constitutional reform of the Empire?
4.2 How strong was the 'Yugoslav' movement?
5   Austro-Russian relations: Why did the Habsburg Empire tend to look to the near east after 1866?
5.1 Why did Austria-Hungary's actions over Bosnia in 1908 annoy Russia?
5.2 What part did Bismarck play in shaping Habsburg foreign policy?
6   Why did the assassination of Franz Ferdinand lead to the outbreak of the First World War? (You may find that it helps to make a brief chronology of the events from 28 June to early August in order to answer this question.)
7   Why did the war lead to the dissolution of the Habsburg Empire? Be aware of the underlying question about whether the dissolution was inevitable or not

Answering essay questions on 'The Habsburg Empire, 1867-1914'

Examination questions on the Habsburg Empire in this period are predominantly about the origins of the First World War. This means, of course, that you should study the roles of the other great powers in the causation of the war. It would be very sensible therefore to use this book in conjunction with *Rivalry and Accord: International Relations 1870-1914* by John Lowe in this series in order to acquire a broader understanding of the causes of the war.

However, there is a very good case for saying that the Great War has its origins in the problems faced by the Habsburgs and so everything is to be gained by studying this book carefully. Indeed, it is precisely the internal problems of the Habsburg Empire that most students answering questions on the First World War fail to understand properly.

Many questions on the origins of the war will approach the question in such a way as to invite an emphasis on the Austro-Hungarian Empire. For example:

1 How far was the Habsburg Empire responsible for the outbreak of the First World War in August 1914?
2 'The First World War was the direct result of Serbian expansionism.' Discuss.
3 How far was Balkan nationalism responsible for causing the First World War?

You should prepare for these sorts of questions by listing the reasons why the Habsburgs might be blamed for the war and the factors which suggest that the wider general war was not of their making. This is a particularly difficult task and indeed the whole question of 'war guilt' is one that has taxed historians since 1918. However, it is very important that you try to arrive at your own idea. Try writing a conclusion to one of the above essays.

Other sorts of questions which may involve a lesser focus on the Habsburg Empire are those that focus on one of the other factors, for example,

4 'The responsibility for the outbreak of the First World War lies firmly with Germany.' Discuss.
5 'The outbreak of the First World War was the result of miscalculation rather than deliberate intent.' Discuss.

Both of these questions will require a section on the role of the Habsburg Empire. Try to write a paragraph in which you discuss whether Germany was more or less guilty than Austria-Hungary.

If the questions are not about the outbreak of the First World war they will probably ask you to assess the problems faced by the Habsburgs after the *Ausgleich*. For example,

6 How effectively did the Habsburg Empire meet the challenges facing it between 1867 and 1913?

This is particularly tricky question. Can you see why? It revolves around the basic question of whether the Empire was doomed to destruction or not. Use this chapter to help you plan an essay in which both views are examined. Again, try to write a conclusion to this question. You will probably find this an extremely difficult task but the very process of wrestling with this question will help you develop and focus your own ideas.

Source-based questions on '*The Habsburg Empire, 1867-1914*'

1 Views of Austrian Democracy.
Carefully read the sources on pages 92-3. Answer the following questions:
a)   In what ways are the descriptions offered by the two different authors similar? (6 marks)
b)   How reliable are these two sources? (4 marks)

2 The Decision to go to War in 1914
Carefully read the sources on page 107 and answer the following questions:
a)   Do these sources support the view that the Habsburg Emperor found it a painful decision to go to war? Justify you answer. (6 marks)
b)   What do you think the Emperor meant by the phrase 'the fates'? (3 marks)
c)   Using these two sources, how would you describe the mood of the Emperor in August 1914? (6 marks)

CHAPTER 6

Interpretations of the History of the Habsburg Empire

1 Introduction

The purpose of this last chapter is to outline the main interpretations of the history of the Habsburg Empire put forward by historians. Broadly speaking there are two dominant interpretations, one of which focuses on the domestic 'nationalities problem' and one which concentrates on 'foreign policy' issues. The main arguments offered by these two schools are explained below.

Although these interpretations are quite different in approach, they agree on their basic conclusion: both argue that the eventual dissolution of the Empire after the Great War had become inevitable much earlier, in the nineteenth century. Thus the dominant overall view of the history of the Habsburg Empire has been, up until quite recently, that the Empire was doomed to self-destruction. However, a new approach to the subject has emerged in recent years which seeks to revise the basic assumption that the collapse of the Empire was inevitable. So-called revisionist historians have disagreed fundamentally with both of the dominant interpretations. The main arguments of the revisionists are laid out in the third section of this chapter. Finally, a fourth section looks at an alternative approach. This seeks to analyse the relationship between cultural developments within the Empire and its eventual demise.

However, it should be remembered that this is only intended to be a brief introduction to the historiography of the subject and not as an alternative to reading the works of the historians discussed.

2 Historical Interpretations

a) The Nationalities Problem

Although historians have explained the Empire's collapse in a number of different ways, almost all have placed a great deal of emphasis on one particular factor: the nationalities problem. This problem is simply stated. The Habsburg Empire was a multi-ethnic political structure, largely assembled at a time before the emergence of popular nationalism. However, in the course of the nineteenth century the peoples of the Empire were increasingly motivated by nationalist feelings. Given that there were at least eleven different national groups within the Empire, it is easy to understand why so many historians have seen the problems of appeasing and containing all the aspirations of these peoples within one political structure as virtually impossible.

Therefore it seems logical to believe that the nationalities problem condemned the Empire to eventual disintegration.

Numerous historians have put forward this view, but one in particular is most associated with it. Oscar Jászi likened nationalism to a centrifugal force which was relentlessly pulling the Empire apart. He argued that the unifying or centripetal forces such as the dynasty itself, the bureaucracy, the army, the church and the aristocracy were insufficiently strong to overcome the growing power of nationalism. In some ways Jászi's interpretation is an extreme one because it rejects the possibility that there may have been some way in which the Habsburgs could have contained and assimilated the nationalism of the peoples of the Empire. Historians like Jászi simply believe that there was no possibility of reconciling the interests of eleven different groups with that of the dynasty. Hence they see the destruction of the Empire as simply a matter of time. The Great War, seen from this perspective, merely accelerated the inevitable.

There is plenty of evidence to support this type of analysis. Most of the major events in the final century of the Monarchy are in some way related to the problems posed by nationalism. Metternich was devoted to the opposition of the national principle wherever he found it. The 1848 revolutions in Bohemia, Italy and Hungary were in large part nationalist revolts. The *Ausgleich* of 1867 was a compromise designed to find a way of appeasing Magyar nationalism. After 1867 much of the rest of the history of the Dual Monarchy is the history of petty nationalist squabbles about the rights of various national groups to use their own language in schools and in dealings with the bureaucracy. And finally. it is often argued that the war which brought about the collapse of the Dual Monarchy was caused by the problems posed by south Slav nationalism in the Balkans. It seems almost self-evident that the later history of the Empire is also the history of the nationalities problem.

But how reasonable is it to regard the nationalities problem as basically insoluble? After all, there were one or two minor successes in reducing tensions between national groups. For example, in February 1914 the antagonism between Poles and Ruthenes in Galicia was considerably reduced when the Poles agreed to allow the Ruthenes much greater representation in the Galician parliament. Of course, this small step forward has tended to be overshadowed by other events in 1914. But for many of the analysts who have argued that the problem was not insoluble the most obvious solution would have been a federal constitution in which each national community had the right to govern itself through a regional assembly whilst also enjoying representation in a central assembly. But the dynasty itself showed little interest in such a radical approach. Only on one occasion was a federal solution seriously put forward. In 1871 Count Hohenwart drew up his proposals to introduce a more federal constitution, giving the Czechs considerable powers of self-government similar to those enjoyed by the Magyars.

Arguably this might have been the beginning of a more fully federalised framework. But, the Magyars and the Bohemian Germans blocked it. After 1871 Franz Joseph showed no more interest in federalism. When in 1918 his successor suggested the idea once more, in a desperate bid to keep the Empire together, the Magyars rejected it again.

There was perhaps only one other solution: to turn the existing dualist system into a democracy, thereby allowing each subject of the Empire the right to express his nationalist feelings through the ballot box. But the Habsburgs found that this solution also foundered on the rock of Magyar obstinacy. When Franz Joseph sought to introduce universal suffrage in Transleithania in 1906 the Magyars aggressively rejected the idea. Magyar supremacy depended upon maintaining a small electorate. They were not willing to agree to anything which threatened their dominant position. However, the Emperor did successfully introduce universal suffrage in Cisleithania in 1907. But, somewhat ironically, this did not so much solve the nationalities problem as exacerbate it. Each ethnic group and sub-group rapidly formed a political party. This created an unstable political life characterised by endless fragile coalitions and alliances. But democracy also introduced other sources of division. Other parties emerged whose identities were shaped partly by national allegiance but also by class or religion, such as the working-class Social Democratic Party or the Roman Catholic Christian Democrats. Thus the nationalities problem became interwoven with the problems of class struggle or sectarian rivalry, all of which created a political system virtually paralysed by its own complexity. Evidently the transition to democracy in the west offered as little hope of resolving the nationalities problem as the lack of democracy did in the east. It is tempting to conclude with Jászi that no solution was possible.

Even more precise arguments can be advanced to support this view. There were very specific reasons why it was so difficult to change the constitution in such a way as to please all national groups. First, it must be admitted that it would have been incredibly difficult to draw up a federal constitution consisting of a patchwork of regional assemblies simply because of the maddening way in which ethnic groups were intermingled. Drawing boundaries around discrete national groups would in many cases have been virtually impossible. There would always have been minority groups trapped within these artificial boundaries. Fortunately or unfortunately, no one had yet thought of the idea of 'ethnic cleansing'. So perhaps a federal solution was simply not practical. Beyond that problem lay a yet more intractable obstacle: the Magyars. There seems little doubt that the *Ausgleich* of 1867, which gave the Magyars an effective veto over any future amendments to the constitution, had effectively petrified the political system. It is therefore tempting to argue that the *Ausgleich* of 1867 finally sealed the fate of the Habsburgs.

But possibly the problem went even deeper than that. The real reason the nationalities problem found no political solution is perhaps that the dynasty did not put much effort into looking for one. Had Franz Joseph energetically sought a federal constitution or indeed an Empire-wide democracy he could perhaps have made it happen, even at the risk of alienating the Magyars. He did not do so because he did not want to do so. The reason for this lies in the Emperor's basic attitude toward his Empire. He did not conceive of the Empire as a device for allowing a community of national groups to live together in peace and harmony: he thought of it simply as the territorial possessions of the house of Habsburg. He was only genuinely interested in short-term political fixes which would enable him to retain, defend and possibly enlarge these territories, which in turn meant that he demanded the right to control foreign policy. In this sense the *Ausgleich* gave him all that he wanted. So the conclusion must be that the interpretation that sees the nationalities problem as condemning the Empire to self-detruction is slightly too simplistic: only the addition of the Emperor's lack of political initiative ensured the eventual disintegration of his Empire.

b) Foreign Policy Errors

Another school of historians, whilst in most cases still regarding the Empire as doomed, has argued that too much emphasis has been placed on the nationalities problem and that the focus of analysis should be more upon foreign policy than on domestic problems. There is much to recommend this approach. To begin with, it does seem that the key foreign policy decisions to go to war at various points in the nineteenth and twentieth centuries led to almost all of the subsequent major changes to the Empire, and indeed to its eventual destruction. The war against Napoleon led to the end of the Holy Roman Empire. The loss of both Lombardy in 1859 and Venetia in 1866 came about as a result of defeats in wars. The foreign policy decision to occupy Bosnia-Herzegovina created the tensions that eventually dragged the Empire into its last war in 1914; a war which brought about the greatest change of all: the demise of the Empire.

This school of historiography has been shaped by one historian more than any other, the great A.J.P. Taylor, particularly in his classic work *The Habsburg Monarchy, 1809-1918* (1948). The Taylor thesis is that the 'fate of the Habsburg Monarchy had been sealed by the war of 1866'. The reasoning behind this sweeping statement is quite complex and requires careful explanation. According to Taylor, defeat in the war against Bismarck's Prussia in 1866 had several devastating consequences. To begin with it established Prussia as the dominant German power and effectively expelled Austria from German affairs. The consequence of this was that the Empire was forced to look to its eastern borders for any further territorial acquisitions. In practice this meant that the Habsburgs began to regard the Balkans as their natural sphere of influence. The pull in this direction was reinforced by the fact that the former dominant power in the Balkans, the Ottoman Empire, had become weak and increasingly vulnerable to predatory Great Powers. This change in the direction of foreign policy appeared to pay dividends in 1878 and 1908 when the Habsburgs occupied and then annexed Bosnia-Herzegovina. However, this acquisition had a sinister side effect. It left Russia feeling resentful and determined to act should Austria ever seek to use force in the Balkans again. Thus the repercussions of defeat in 1866 could be said to have created the scenario which eventually precipitated the Balkan war of 1914 which became the Great War.

But Taylor and his admirers go further than this. They argue that the defeat of 1866 indirectly created a curious double dependency; the Habsburgs rapidly found themselves dependent first upon the Magyars, as a result of the *Ausgleich* of 1867, and then ironically upon Germany. The latter dependency was formalised in 1879 when Andrássy formed an alliance with Germany. In other words, as an indirect result of 1866, Austria came to be fatally dependent on the goodwill of Germany and Hungary. The consequence of this double dependency, though not immediately apparent, was to be the end of the Empire. The Magyars, as we have seen, would not allow any internal reforms to the Empire. But more importantly, according to Taylor, the Germans came to control Habsburg foreign policy in such a way as to ensure the destruction of the Empire. His case is that, although it was certainly the Habsburgs who took the decision to go to war with Serbia in 1914, after the murder of Franz Ferdinand, the Habsburgs rapidly lost control of their own destiny after the war had begun. The German Schlieffen Plan turned the Balkan war into a major European War, plunging the Austro-Hungarian Empire into a war with Britain and France, the former of which had been an unofficial supporter of the Empire for years. But the full consequences of the fatal dependency upon Germany only became apparent in 1915. By this time the Austrian army had been defeated so often that, as Taylor says, 'by every analogy of Habsburg history, this would have been the moment to make peace'. As in 1859 and 1866 the Habsburgs could have withdrawn and accepted some minor territorial losses. The reason this did not happen was that the Austrian army was 'saved' by the German army. German generals reversed the defeats of 1915 and effectively took over the runnning of the Austrian war effort. By the end of 1915 Franz Joseph was no longer in control of his armies. Dependency upon Germany had now become explicit: Austria-Hungary was being dragged behind a mighty German military machine determined upon the mastery of Europe. Prevented from finding a way out of the war, the Empire's fate now depended entirely upon German success. The defeat of Germany in 1918 spelled the end of the Habsburg Monarchy. All of this, according to Taylor, was the indirect but inevitable result of the Emperor's disastrous decision to go to war in 1866.

Alhough we might not accept Taylor's case in its entirety, there is clearly some truth in the view that foreign policy decisions rather than internal tensions between nationalities caused the downfall of the Empire. Of course, it may be possible to reconcile these two interpretations as they are not mutually exclusive. Foreign and domestic policies did not exist entirely separate from one another. For example, there seems little doubt that the decision to go to war with Serbia in 1914 was motivated by the worries about disaffected Bosnian Serbs within the Empire. Foreign policy decisions were always greatly influenced by domestic considerations. Thus, in a sense the two dominant interpretations reinforce each other and both convey one message above all: that the Empire was always heading towards destruction. If this 'bipartisan' view is accepted, it is, of course, necessary for each student to make his or her own assessment of the relative significance of the two factors.

c) The Revisionist Interpretation

In recent years a new school of historians have begun to question the assumptions behind the two dominant interpretations. Of those writing in English, the leading voice is historian Alan Sked - see his informed study *The Decline and Fall of the Habsburg Empire, 1815-1918* (1989). Above all, revisionists such as Sked have challenged the idea that the Empire was doomed. They argue that, in general, nationalism was not a centrifugal force threatening to dissolve the Empire. In particular they reject the notion that Slav nationalism, most historians' choice as the chief solvent of dynastic loyalties, was somehow bound to break the Empire apart. For example, revisionist historians have pointed out that the Czechs, who were one of the most nationalist and disaffected Slav groups, did not call for the abolition of the Empire; they called for a federal reform of the Empire. Only in the last years of the war did Czech nationalists become separatists. Before 1914, the revisionists argue, there was nothing about the Czech problem which made the destruction of the Empire inevitable. Furthermore, they have shown that other Slav groups such as the Poles and Croats enjoyed certain rights of self-government within the political structure of the Empire, a fact which tended to make them supporters of the existing constitution rather than opponents of it. Indeed far from being a centrifugal force relentlessly pulling the Empire apart, according to the revisionists, nationalism was not really a threat to the existence of the Empire at all. To quote Sked, 'the truth is that there was no internal pressure between 1867 and 1914 for the break up of the Monarchy'.

When it comes to the events of 1914, the revisionists continue to run against the grain. They reject the view that Princip's assassination of

Franz Ferdinand was an expression of south Slav nationalist feeling. The problem with the traditional argument, they claim, is that it assumes that Gavrilo Princip was acting with the support of Bosnian Serbs and possibly with other south Slav groups such as the Croats and Slovenes. But the evidence assembled by revisionists largely contradicts this. It seems that Princip, like most assassins, was an isolated and slightly pathetic figure. In shooting the heir to the throne he did not act for the Bosnian Serbs in the Empire. In fact, he was the instrument of a foreign terrorist organisation, the Black Hand, which in turn was supported, albeit covertly, by the Serbian government. In other words, it could be argued that it was forces *outside* of the Empire itself which precipitated the crisis of 1914. The assassination of Franz Ferdinand can therefore be viewed not as a bloody expression of insurmountable ethnic tensions within the Empire but as an attack by a hostile and predatory neighbour. As for the idea that Princip may have had the support of the Croats and Slovenes, again the evidence points the other way. Despite the creation of the Kingdom of Serbs, Croats, and Slovenes in 1920 (only renamed Yugoslavia in 1928) it does not seem that there was an overwhelming movement pressing for the creation of such a state before 1914. Instead, the peoples of the Balkans - the Serbs, the Croats and the Bosnian Muslims - were more interested in the rivalries existing between themselves than in any unified opposition to the Habsburgs.

Perhaps the most convincing evidence of all against the idea that the peoples of the Empire were impatient for the break-up of the Empire lies in the simple fact that these same peoples fought in the Imperial armies throughout most of the war with an extraordinary degree of loyalty. It might be objected that these peoples had very little choice, but even so, if nationalism was indeed a centrifugal force destined to fling the nationalities into their separate states, there would surely have been more mutinies and wilful defeatism.

It is tempting to conclude that the revisionists must be correct and that the emergence of nationalism did not necessarily make the collapse of the Empire inevitable. However, one or two questions remain. In particular the revisionists have not been able adequately to explain how the constitution might ever have been modified, given the existing veto enjoyed by the Magyars as a result of the *Ausgleich*. It is hard to see how the Empire could have reformed its constitution in such a way as to give the various subject peoples a share of power, without prompting a Hungarian revolt which would probably have meant the break-up of the Empire. The fact that the Magyars still objected to constitutional change during the last two years of the war, when the collapse of the Empire became a real threat and only a federal constitution might have ensured the loyalty of the various Slav groups, is surely proof that the Magyars would never have given up their opposition to constitutional reform. It therefore seems logical to conclude that only complete destruction of the dualist mould and therefore of the entire Empire could offer the subjugated subjects of the Monarchy a chance of self-government.

As will be clear by now, the idea that the nationalities problem made the dissolution of the Empire inevitable is highly debatable. The revisionists have provided a useful corrective to some of the more simplistic assumptions about Habsburg history, but it is apparent that they have overstated this part of their case.

The revisionists have also attacked the second dominant interpretation: the view that foreign policy errors determined the course of Imperial history long before 1914. In particular, the Taylor thesis that all was lost after the battle of Sadowa has come under attack. Revisionists admit that 1866 may have been a profoundly significant defeat but suggest that the subsequent alliance with Germany in 1879 can hardly be seen as marking an obvious point of no return. They point out that Bismarck, probably the main architect of the alliance, sought to use it to prevent war, and that, more to the point, this very alliance actually did prevent war in 1908 over the annexation of Bosnia by the Empire, when Austro-German solidarity forced Russia to back down. The fact that it had exactly the opposite effect in 1914 could hardly have been predicted.

Indeed, the revisionists argue that not only was dissolution entirely unpredictable in 1866, 1879, or 1908, but also that it was not seen as very likely even as late as 1917. They contend that the destruction of the Empire came about largely because the Americans were in a position to dictate the shape of the peace in 1918, and because their president, Woodrow Wilson, was a firm believer in the nation state and was ideologically opposed to dynastic Empires. The British and French had not set out to dissolve the Empire, in fact both powers tended to regard the great Empire as something which helped to keep stability in central Europe by preventing the continent from descending into a myriad of national rivalries. Only in the last months of the war did British and French opinion swing towards the idea of dismembering the Empire. In other words, revisionists argue that the break-up of the Empire was a largely unforeseen twist of circumstances, determined by the immediate needs of a handful of western leaders rather than the inevitable outcome of a chain of foreign policy decisions.

Overall, the main thrust of revisionist analysis then is that there was nothing inevitable about the fate of the Empire. It should not be thought of as sliding remorselessly towards historical oblivion. As Sked argues, 'the fact that the Monarchy fell does not logically have to imply any decline at all'. Indeed, as Sked himself concludes, the simple truth is that 'it fell because it lost a major war'.

3 An Alternative Approach: The Cultural Interpretation

Although the historiography of the demise of the Habsburg Empire has tended to revolve around either the nationalities problem or foreign policy, one or two historians, such as W.M. Johnson in his study *The Austrian Mind: an Intellectual and Social History* (1972) have looked instead at cultural developments within the Empire. Between 1890 and 1918 Vienna became the centre of an extraordinary explosion of cultural activity. Although it is notoriously difficult to define cultural movements, it is broadly accurate to argue that the main idea behind this intellectual revolt was the belief that almost all existing values, ideas and assumptions had to be questioned. Some historians have judged that these cultural upheavals were corroding the very foundations of Austrian society. Hence it has been argued that the Habsburg Empire was fatally weakened by a decadent and pessimistic intellectual revolution. But how much truth is there in such a view?

It is certainly true that what might be called solid bourgeois, Christian values were under assault in *fin de siècle* Vienna. Perhaps the most profound attack on traditional values was that posed by the ideas of Sigmund Freud. Working in Vienna at the turn of the century Freud was well known in Austrian intellectual circles and his ideas were extremely influential. According to Freud all human behaviour could be related to certain 'unconscious' impulses, most of which were conditioned by the sexual drive. Man was revealed as basically irrational and amoral. Even

Death and Life 1908, by Gustav Klimt

God could be explained away in terms of unconscious drives and needs. Freud's ideas may no longer seem revolutionary to us, but to the respectable pillars of Viennese society such thoughts were profoundly shocking. Simultaneously painters such as Klimt, Schiele and Kokoschka portrayed the human body in rather disturbing ways, dwelling on themes such as dreams, sexual desire and death. This corrosive culture also made itself felt in the dramatic and musical arts. Schnitzler's play *La Ronde* depicted apparently respectable bourgeois figures as sexual hypocrites. Mahler's symphonies with their sudden shifts from the ecstatic to the despairing might be thought the perfect soundtrack to the last tragic years of a doomed world.

Indeed the intellectual revolution was so successful in destroying traditional values that many thoughtful young men and women were left with a sense of pointlessness or futility. It is not a coincidence that turn of the century Austria-Hungary had an unusually high rate of suicide. The most famous case of all occurred in 1889 at the hunting lodge of Crown Prince Rudolf, the thirty-one year old heir to the throne. In mysterious circumstances the Crown Prince shot first his teenage mistress and then himself. The precise reasons for this bizarre elopement into eternity are obscure but Rudolf was not alone in seeing no point in going on. The intellectual elite in the Empire seemed unified in despair, and this mood reached the very highest levels of society. Even the Emperor himself regarded the future with a grim fatalism, writing to his mother that 'one just has to resist as long as possible, do one's duty to the last and finally perish with honour'. It was almost as if the Empire itself believed its own demise was inevitable, which in turn became a self-fulfilling prophecy.

But, how significant is all this cultural giddiness? How much weight should historians place on this factor when considering the reasons for the downfall of the Empire?

It is certainly possible to see the despairing side of this movement as in some ways a reflection of the Empire's own bleak future: as artistic and intellectual evidence for the inevitability of the death of the Empire. Perhaps the Empire also committed suicide. But this is too glib, too simplistic. A number of caveats must be entered against this seductive thesis.

It could surely equally well be argued that such an outpouring of talent is a testament to the freedom and cosmopolitanism of Viennese life. At the very least, we must be aware that such creativity could just as easily be seen as a mark of the vitality of the Empire as an indication of its degeneration. And, even if it is accepted that this cultural effusion was destructive and corrosive of traditional society, it should be remembered that so-called 'modernist' culture was not unique to the Empire; almost every large sophisticated city in western Europe attracted such artists. Paris was perhaps the most subversive city in Europe but France as a whole was largely untouched by the ferment. The same point can be made with more force about the Austro-Hungarian Empire. The vast majority of subjects of the Monarchy were not part of this movement. The largest single class in the Empire was still the peasantry, who had very little use on the farm for the ideas of Freud. The same might be said for the millions of provincial people of all classes who never ventured into Vienna nor took much notice of its fleeting intellectual fashions. In short, we must be very careful before claiming that events in the arts are reliable predictors of future developments in politics.

4 Assessment

It may be, then, that the dissolution of the Habsburg Empire was not inevitable. History has now taught us that the new states that emerged out of the ruins of the Empire, the so-called successor states such as Czechoslovakia and Yugoslavia, were no more rational or stable than the Monarchy itself. Nationalism, assumed by so many western thinkers, such as Woodrow Wilson, to be preferable to dynasticism, has shown itself to be capable of far greater horrors than anything perpetrated by the Habsburgs. In fact, the history of post-Habsburg central and eastern Europe has been so scarred by the violence of Fascism and Communism and post-Communist ethnic wars, that historians have been tempted to indulge in a little sentimentality towards the Habsburgs, perhaps even to see the fall of the Monarchy as a tragic mishap in which the Habsburgs were the unfortunate victims of forces beyond their control.

But this is to allow nostalgia to cloud one's judgement. There was indeed nothing inevitable about the end of the Empire. It might have resolved its problems, but it chose not to try to do so. In 1914 Franz Joseph chose war as his preferred solution to the problems posed by Balkan nationalism. In that sense the end of the Empire came about as a result of its inability to find better solutions: a kind of failure of the political imagination. Franz Joseph had no blueprint for the future, only a series of schemes for defending the past. (He would not adopt new inventions such as the telephone or the typewriter.) In the final analysis this reflects the fact that the Achilles heel of the Austro-Hungarian Empire was its almost complete dependence upon the abilities, or otherwise, of the ruling Emperor. Though this is true of most powerful monarchical systems, this was even more marked in Austria-Hungary because loyalty to the Habsburgs was the only serious idea holding the Empire together. As A.J.P. Taylor put it memorably, 'in other countries dynasties are episodes in the history of the people; in the Habsburg Empire peoples are a complication in the history of the dynasty.'

In the last analysis the people were there to serve the state and the state was always just one man. It is therefore tempting to see the final demise of the Empire as the simple consequence of an old man's mistake. But this would be to ignore the fact that the decisions of this one man were largely determined by the extraordinary pressures, both internal and external, acting upon him.

Furthermore, despite the attractiveness of Taylor's paradox, the history of the Habsburg Empire cannot be reduced to one man or indeed one thesis. Above all else the Habsburg Empire was a complex affair and a subject that defies easy generalisations. Perhaps the only thing upon which historians of the Habsburg state have really agreed, is that it was, to an almost absurd extent, an Empire of contradictions.

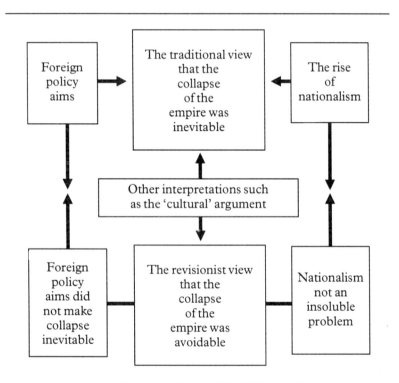

Summary - Interpretations of the History of the Habsburg Empire

Working on *'Interpretations of the History of the Habsburg Empire'*

When you have finished reading this chapter and examining the summary diagram it is to be hoped that you will have a clear understanding of the four different arguments outlined above. In order to test whether you have grasped the points and are able to articulate them lucidly you should briefly answer the following questions.

1   Explain why some historians feel that the multi-ethnic nature of the Empire doomed it to destruction.

2 Explain how it might be argued that foreign policy mistakes locked the Empire on course for destruction.
3 List the points that might be made to defend the view that the dissolution of the Empire was not inevitable.
4 Explain how it might be argued that cultural developments around the turn of the century fatally undermined the Empire.

When you are able to answer the above questions you will be in a position, if appropriate, to deepen your understanding by reading the works of some of the outstanding historians mentioned.

Chronological Table

1806	Abdication of Francis II as Holy Roman Emperor and effective end of the Holy Roman Empire
	Francis II became Francis I of Austria
1809	Metternich appointed Foreign Minister
1815	Congress of Vienna
	Holy Alliance drawn up by Tsar Alexander I
	Quadruple Alliance
1818	Congress of Aix-la-Chapelle
1819	Karlsbad Decrees
1820-1	Revolts in Spain, Naples, Portugal, Piedmont and Greece led to the Congresses of Troppau and Laibach and the Troppau Protocol
1822	Congress of Verona. Collapse of the Congress System
1828-9	Russo-Turkish War
1830	Greek independence
	Revolution in France
1835	Death of Francis I, accession of Ferdinand I
1840	Mehemet Ali Crisis
1848	24 February, Abdication of Louis Philippe in France
	13 March, Resignation of Metternich
	11 April, Ferdinand approved the 'April Laws'
	15 May, Second uprising in Vienna
	2 June, Pan-Slav Congress opened in Prague
	28 June, Windischgraetz ruthlessly suppressed Pan-Slav Congress
	25 July, Radetzky defeated Piedmont at Custozza, re-entered Milan
	11 September, Jellačić invaded Hungary
	6 October, Third uprising in Vienna
	31 October, Windischgraetz crushed the Vienna revolution
	2 December, Abdication of Ferdinand: accession of Franz Joseph
1849	7 March, Reichstag at Kremsier dissolved
	13 August, Hungarians defeated at Vilagòs
	28 August, Venice surrendered
1851	31 December, Sylvester Patent restored absolutism
1860	20 October, October Diploma
1866	Austria defeated by Prussia at Sadowa (Königgrätz)

1867	Austro-Hungarian Compromise or *Ausgleich*
1878	Congress of Berlin: occupation of Bosnia-Herzegovina
1879	Austria-Hungary allied with Germany in Dual Alliance
1897	Badeni Crisis
1907	Universal Suffrage introduced in Austria
1908	Bosnia-Herzegovina annexed
1914	28 June, Franz Ferdinand assassinated at Sarajevo
	5 July, Germany gave unconditional support to Austria-Hungary in the so-called 'blank cheque'
	28 July Austria-Hungary declared war on Serbia. Partial mobilisation by Russia
	1-4 August, Germany declared war on Russia, France and Belgium. Britain declared war on Germany
1915	Italy declared war on Austria-Hungary
1916	Death of Franz Joseph
1917	America entered the war against the Central Powers
1918-19	Defeat and Dissolution

Further Reading

There are relatively few accessible books on the Habsburg Empire suitable for students. However, listed below are those works which are recommended reading for anyone seeking to achieve the highest examination grades in this subject.

A. Sked, *The Decline and Fall of the Habsburg Empire, 1815-1918* (Longman, 1989). This book is easily the best single volume to emerge on the subject in the relatively recent past. It assumes a fair amount of basic knowledge, but has the great merit of steering the reader through the maze of historiographical interpretation whilst also offering a stimulating revisionist perspective of its own.

C.A. Macartney, *The Habsburg Empire, 1790-1918* (Weidenfeld and Nicolson, 1969). This text still remains the best source of factual information on the subject. However, it is probably too detailed for a student fresh to the subject. Macartney does not discriminate between the important and the not so important, so use the index to look up what you want.

A.J.P. Taylor, *The Habsburg Monarchy, 1809-1918* (Penguin, 1948). Although this is now a rather ancient work, it is undoubtedly a classic; possibly the greatest work of one of Britain's greatest historians. It is almost worth reading for the entertainment alone. At the least, you should dip into it. It is a rich mine of short, snappy quotations.

E. Crankshaw, *The Fall of the House of Habsburg* (Papermac, 1981). This tells the story of the dynasty very effectively and with a great deal of sympathy.

A. Sked (ed), *Europe's Balance of Power* (Macmillan, 1979). This is particularly good on the age of Metternich and his supposed system.

J.W. Mason, *The Dissolution of the Habsburg Empire* (Longman Seminar Studies, 1985). This is a reliable guide to the Empire after 1867, with the added advantage of a collection of primary sources at the end.

M. Cornwall (ed), *The Last Years of Austria-Hungary* (University of Exeter Press, 1990). This is a specialist study of the years between 1908 and 1918. It is very detailed but will repay close study.

J. Lowe, *Rivalry and Accord: International Relations 1870-1914* (Arnold, 1988). Good basic guide to the wider European situation.

S.R. Williamson, *Austria-Hungary and the Origins of the First World War* (Macmillan, 1991). Excellent study of this complex question.

A. Palmer, *The Twilight of the Habsburgs* (Weidenfeld and Nicolson, 1994). Although basically a biography of Franz Joseph, it is wonderfully detailed and covers a great deal of ground.

Index